THE PREVALENCE OF CHILD SEXUAL ABUSE IN BRITAIN

A feasibility study for a large-scale national survey of the general population

DEBORAH GHATE LIZ SPENCER

Social and Community Planning Research

STUDIES IN CHILD PROTECTION

LONDON: HMSO

Applications for reproduction should be made to HMSO Copyright Unit
First published 1995
Second Impression

ISBN 0 11 321783 8

Acknowledgements

We would like to thank our colleagues at Social and Community Planning Research for their help on this study: Bob Erens for technical advice on quantitative aspects of the project; Jill Keegan and Kit Ward for conducting interviews during the qualitative phase.

Contents

TABLES

FIGURES

Introduction

A developmental study, addressing the feasibility of a large scale national survey of the prevalence of child sexual abuse, was commissioned by the Department of Health and carried out by Social and Community Planning Research during 1991–1993. This report documents the work and conclusions of that study.

Genesis of the study

Although concern about the sexual abuse of children had been growing since the late 1970s among doctors, therapists, and professionals working in the field of child protection, widescale public attention only started to be attracted in this country during the 1980s. Public debate was triggered by a number of newspaper articles and television programmes, but particularly by the publicity which surrounded the events in Cleveland in 1987. In addition to questions about how the Cleveland cases should have been handled, issues were raised about the extent to which child sexual abuse was increasing in scale or simply more readily identified and reported.

The Report of the Inquiry into Child Abuse in Cleveland (Butler-Sloss, 1988) documented many of the difficulties of identifying and monitoring abuse. In particular, the report highlighted the absence of reliable estimates of incidence or prevalence in this country, and recommended that some attention be given to measuring the scale of the problem (Recommendation 1, p245). Reliable information was felt to be important in order for services in the field of diagnosis, support, and prevention to be planned.[1]

In response to public and political concern, and as part of a larger programme of research on child protection, the Department of Health commissioned a feasibility study for a national survey of the prevalence of child sexual abuse.

Prevalence or incidence?

For a number of ethical and methodological reasons a study of prevalence was proposed, to estimate the proportion of adults who have experienced sexual abuse during childhood, rather than a study of incidence estimating the number of cases per year. It was not in the remit of the study to evaluate the relative merits of prevalence versus incidence studies in any detail;

---

[1] Such planning could only be based, however, on estimates of incidence or prevalence for the population as a whole, requiring a survey of the general population rather than one based on clinical or other special populations, and a random rather than quota sample. (See Section 4 of this report)

however, the arguments in favour of a prevalence study are summarised briefly here. Firstly, estimates of incidence are usually based on the number of cases known to professionals such as doctors, therapists, social workers, or the police. As such, even the most rigorous studies which combine reports across multiple agencies (e.g. Royal Belfast Hospital and Queen's University 1990) represent only those cases which have been identified or reported. Since as Finkelhor (1986) has said, the tabooed nature of abuse inhibits discovery and discourages reporting, known cases cannot be taken as indicative of the total number of cases in the population as a whole. Indeed, estimates of incidence gathered in this way have been described as representing only the tip of a very large iceberg (Finkelhor 1986, La Fontaine 1990, Rush 1980). On the other hand, alternative methodologies for establishing incidence, such as a national survey amongst children, are considered to pose insuperable ethical dilemmas at present. Although prevalence studies are retrospective rather than indicative of current levels of abuse and subject to a number of different constraints, they nevertheless provide an opportunity to estimate past and relatively recent levels of child sexual abuse among the population as a whole, and to evaluate changes in levels over time. Since the data they provide are drawn from community samples, they are likely to provide a somewhat different view of child sexual abuse than that generated by clinical studies alone. For example, it is likely that they will uncover cases of abuse which are less likely to come to the attention of the child protection agencies. This might be because such cases represent a form of abuse which is not generally recognised or thought to exist; because the abuse has not had observable consequences for, or effects on, the child (or those effects were not recognised as resulting from abuse); or because they occurred in families or communities insulated from the attentions of outsiders. Although subject to their own biases and limitations, prevalence studies theoretically provide estimates closer to a "true" rate than do incidence studies. Thus many professionals, researchers and clinicians working in this field consider that an authoritative British prevalence study would be of great value.

Current prevalence estimates

The decision to commission a feasibility study prior to committing resources to a full-scale national survey was based on a number of reservations about existing prevalence estimates, and concerns about the methodological and ethical issues which would need to be resolved before a large scale survey could take place.

In practice, although a number of prevalence studies have been carried out in the United States, few studies have been conducted in this country. British research to date has included: studies based on 'accessibility' sampling such as patients from a GP practice (Nash and West 1985), and college students (Kelly et al. 1991); "volunteer" studies among magazine readers and television viewers (Koshal 1986) and a national study conducted by MORI (Baker and Duncan 1985). With each of these studies there have been questions about the size or composition of sample, or about the definitions adopted, and consequently about the generalisability and comparability of the findings.

Indeed, the lack of comparability between studies is a feature of both the British and American research, where a wide diversity in prevalence estimates can be found, ranging from 5% to 62% for women and 3% to 27% for men. Much of this discrepancy can be attributed to differences of definition and methodology. In particular, as several authors have argued (Russell 1984; Finkelhor 1986; Wyatt and Peters 1986a; Haugaard and Reppucci 1988; Widom 1988; Kelly et al. 1991), the way in which child sexual abuse is defined and operationalised has a dramatic effect on prevalence estimates, with narrower definitions producing lower overall rates. Not all the discrepancy, however, can be ascribed to definitions alone; a number of other aspects of design, such as the type of sample, the number and nature of questions asked to elicit details of sexual abuse, and the mode of administration have all been shown to influence the estimates of prevalence identified. (Finkelhor 1986; Wyatt and Peters 1986b; Widom 1988; Vizard 1989)

Aims and scope of the study

With these discrepancies and general lack of comparability in mind, the feasibility study set out to address a number of methodological, procedural and ethical issues. These issues are outlined in more detail in **Section 1**, and are discussed in full in the remainder of this report. Broadly speaking, these include:

- case definition: whether and how to define child sexual abuse
- context, approach, and presentation: how to present the study in general, and questions on child sexual abuse in particular
- response rates and bias
- the size, type, and composition of the sample
- questionnaire design
- mode of administration
- memory and recall
- interviewer preparation and training
- confidentiality and ethics

Design and conduct of the study

Because of the sensitive and challenging nature of the study, a developmental, incremental approach was adopted, consisting of a number of phases of research, each building upon the findings and lessons of the last. These phases included: a familiarisation stage; early unstructured interviews with known survivors[2] and members of the general public; semi-structured interviews including examples of questionnaire modules; and structured interviews using a fully developed questionnaire. A combination of qualitative and quantitative methods was adopted throughout, with testing and feedback at each stage. A total of 25 depth interviews and 127 survey interviews was carried out.

Familiarisation

Phase 1

The purpose of this initial phase was to consult with professionals, practitioners, and academics working in the field of child sexual abuse, and to review the existing literature.[3] In particular, the familiarisation phase was designed to evaluate the nature of child sexual abuse; theories as to its occurrence; profiles of the characteristics of victims and perpetrators; features of the disclosure process; and the short and long term effects of abusive experiences. From a methodological standpoint, other studies were examined with regard to their estimates of prevalence, and in relation to aspects of their chosen methodology, such as questionnaire design and the definition and overall approach adopted. Phase 1 was carried out between November 1991 and February 1992.

---

[2] Throughout this report we use the term "survivors" to refer to adults who identify themselves as having been sexually abused in childhood. For the purposes of this report the term can be regarded as interchangable with "victim", but is used in particular to refer to the people with whom we made contact through counselling and self-help organisations. These people expressed a preference for the term survivor as a more positive and optimistic label than that of victim.

[3] We are most grateful to the following people who kindly gave up their time to discuss the study with us, and whose contributions have been invaluable: Elizabeth Monck (Institute of Child Health, London); Professor Jean La Fontaine (London School of Economics and Political Science); Ray Wyre (Gracewell Institute); Dr Marjorie Smith (Thomas Coram Institute); Dr Jill Hodges and Dr David Skuse (Great Ormond Street Hospital); Chris Cherry and Julian Turner (Off Centre); Charmian Richardson (Bedfordshire Rape Crisis); Lorraine Waterhouse (Department of Social Administration, University of Edinburgh); Professor Jean Golding (Department of Child Health, University of Bristol); Valerie Howarth and Hereward Harrison (Childline); Dr Eileen Vizard (Tavistock Clinic); Dr Liz Kelly and colleagues (University of North London); Dr David Finkelhor (Family Research Laboratory, University of New Hampshire); Sara Scott (Broadcasting Support Services); Katrin Andersson and Dr Cathy Roberts (SCOSAC).

Unstructured interviews

Phase 2

Phase 2 consisted of 20 unstructured depth interviews, designed to further our understanding of the complexities of child sexual abuse, and of approaching the general public on such a sensitive topic. Thirteen of these initial interviews were with known adult survivors of child sexual abuse, networked through a number of counselling organisations, and 7 were with members of the general population, randomly selected according to simple socio-demographic quotas for age, gender and social class.

The process of recruiting and interviewing adult survivors constituted a major part of this study, providing valuable insights into how a national survey might be perceived by people who have experienced sexual abuse in childhood. A discussion held among a group of survivors indicated initial reservations about the feasibility of such a study, but strong support for wider acknowledgment of and better information about the problem. Despite this initial scepticism, members of this group were willing to be interviewed individually and at considerable length, with interviews lasting from 2 to over 4 hours. Broadly speaking, interviews with these and other survivors provided important information regarding: the complexity of individual stories and experiences; the diversity of individual responses to abusive experiences; and feedback on survivors' reactions to both the idea of a national survey and to the interview process itself.[4] A total of 9 women and 4 men took part, ranging in age from 22 to 54. A wide range of experiences was recounted, ranging from father-daughter incest over a number of years to a single incident of rape.

Interviews with the general population sample were aimed at testing public reactions, and were used to try out a number of different introductions and rationales for the study. A total of 4 women and 3 men took part, ranging in age from 23 to 48. Childhood sexual experiences among this group consisted for the most part of consensual and exploratory games, or petting with girlfriends and boyfriends, though some cases of exhibitionism were also reported. Phase 2 interviews were conducted between March and May 1992.

Semi-structured and structured pre-pilot interviews

Phase 3 : pre-pilots 1–3

Because of the sensitivity of the material, and the difficulty of producing a structured instrument which would do justice to the complexity of the

---

[4] A copy of the Topic Guide, covering the issues addressed in these interviews, can be found in the Technical Appendix.

subject, it was decided to move in stages from a loosely structured questionnaire to a more structured one using a modular approach in which new
modules could be phased in and old ones retained or phased out as necessary.
During this stage, insights gained from the familiarisation phase and from the
depth interviews were used to help devise a research questionnaire which was
modified over the course of the pre-pilots carried out between June and
September 1992.

In addition to evolving a structured questionnaire, these pre-pilots were
designed to evaluate ways of presenting the study to the public, and a number
of different approaches were used at this stage. A further consideration was
the need to "phase in" SCPR field interviewers to work alongside the
research team, gradually taking over responsibility for the interviewing task.
Eight of the most experienced SCPR field interviewers were introduced to
the study throughout this stage.

Finally, sampling methods moved from quota to probability sampling
during Phase 3. In **pre-pilots 1 and 2**, 41 respondents were recruited
according to quotas based on age, gender, marital status and childhood social
class (i.e. parent's occupation). In **pre-pilot 3**, however, a random sample of
pre-selected addresses replaced the quota samples of the previous two pre-
pilots, and 38 respondents were recruited to take part.

Phase 4 : pre-pilot 4

As the final stage of the feasibility study, Phase 4 was designed to be the
"dress rehearsal" for the full scale pilot study which would be required before
a national survey could go into to field. Based on the information gained
from the previous phases, the preferred approach and sampling method were
selected, and a fully structured questionnaire was drawn up and used with a
pre-selected random sample of addresses in six different parts of the country.
A total of 48 productive interviews was achieved in this pre-pilot.

Follow-up interviews were also carried out with a small number of
respondents chosen to represent a range of socio-demographic characteristics
and sexual experiences in childhood. The purpose of these interviews was to
investigate in more detail respondents' perceptions of the survey and the
process of being interviewed, as well as to explore issues such as quality and
accuracy of recall. A total of 5 depth interviews of this type was carried out at
this stage. Phase 4 was conducted during October and November 1992.

The Technical Appendix to this report gives a more detailed account of
the design, content and conduct of the various stages in the study.

Structure of this report

The report below outlines the procedures adopted throughout this
developmental study, and describes our findings and conclusions vis à vis the

approaches adopted. **Section 1** reviews the methodological and ethical issues to be addressed in a study of this kind. **Section 2** considers alternative contexts and approaches for presenting the study to the general public. **Section 3** considers the issue of response and reports on the findings of the four pre-pilot studies. Sampling is the subject of **Section 4**; and questionnaire design is discussed in detail in **Section 5**. **Section 6** considers alternative modes of administration for the fully structured questionnaire. **Section 7** discusses memory and recall and considers strategies for triggering and locating childhood memories. Interviewer requirements and training are the subject of **Section 8**. **Section 9** reviews the issues of confidentiality and ethics, particularly in relation to a study of this nature. Finally, **Section 10** draws together the overall findings of the feasibility study, and discusses the implications for a national prevalence study.

Key issues to be addressed

As discussed in the previous section, in order to assess the feasibility of conducting a large scale national survey of the prevalence of child sexual abuse a number of methodological, procedural and ethical issues had to be addressed during the course of the development study. Generally speaking, these concerned overall questions of definition, and detailed considerations concerning the design and implementation of the survey.

Case definition

An initial issue for consideration was the way in which child sexual abuse should be defined for the study, and how such a definition should be operationalised so as to achieve comparability with other studies. Comparability, however, is hampered by the fact that in the literature there is no consensus about what constitutes child sexual abuse, as the following examples illustrate.

> *Sexual abuse is defined as the involvement of dependent, developmentally immature children and adolescents in sexual activities they do not truly comprehend, to which they do not give informed consent, or that violates the taboos of family roles.*
> (Kempe and Kempe 1978)

> *The sexual abuse of children refers primarily to the activities of adults who use children for their sexual gratification ..... 'sexual abuse' refers to bodily contact of all sorts: fondling, genital stimulation, oral and/or anal intercourse as well as vaginal intercourse. Some people may extend the meaning to include suggestive behaviour, sexual innuendo or exhibitionism (flashing).*
> (La Fontaine 1990)

As far as prevalence studies are concerned, a number of different approaches to definition have been adopted. In some of the early studies, for example, no clear definition of child sexual abuse was specified, either in terms of the behaviour considered to be 'sexual', or the ages considered to represent 'childhood' (Hamilton 1929; Landis 1956; Walters 1975). In other studies, by contrast, child sexual abuse is defined at the outset or an operational definition can be inferred from the range of questions asked. Where either theoretical or operational definitions are identified, however, they can be based on quite different, and sometimes contradictory conditions.

In general, definitions of child sexual abuse tend to vary according their assumptions regarding:

- the type of activity to be included
- the age of the victim/survivor
- an age differential between abuser and abused
- the nature of the relationship between abuser and abused
- the issue of consent/responsibility/legality

Type of activity

In some definitions of child sexual abuse the nature of the activities referred to are key criteria for defining abuse. Among these, sexual abuse may be restricted to bodily contact of some kind such as fondling or intercourse (Briere and Runtz 1988; Siegal et al. 1987), or may also include non-contact behaviour such as exhibitionism, sexual propositioning, or innuendo (Finkelhor 1979, 1984, Finkelhor et al. 1990; Nash and West 1985; Haugaard and Emery 1989; Russell 1984; Wyatt 1985; Baker and Duncan 1985; Kelly et al. 1991). Other definitions, however, leave the nature of the behaviour unspecified, and may concentrate on related contextual aspects of a sexual encounter which are considered pertinent. These might include the age of the victim, presence or absence of informed consent, or the cultural or legal appropriateness of any form of sexual behaviour involving children (Kempe and Kempe 1978).

Age of victim/survivor

Setting an age limit to the period considered to be 'childhood' is a key component of many definitions of child sexual abuse. The choice of age limit may be determined according to legal considerations such as the age of consent, or the age of majority, or alternatively may reflect stages of physical and sexual maturity. For the most part, the cut-off point for childhood is set at 16, and prevalence rates refer to sexual experiences before a person reaches this age (Finkelhor 1979; Nash and West 1985; Baker and Duncan 1985; Siegal et al. 1987). In other studies the age limit is placed at 18 (Russell 1984; Badgely et al. 1984; Lewis 1985; Kelly et al. 1991), or alternatively reduced to 15 (Briere and Runtz 1988). In a few studies, however, definitions of child sexual abuse are confined to pre-pubertal sexual experiences (Landis 1956; Fritz et al. 1981).

Age differential between abuser and abused

In addition to the age of the person abused, definitions of child sexual abuse also tend to assume a difference in age, maturity and responsibility between the abuser and the abused. In some cases, reference is made simply to sexual experiences between children and adults (Kempe and Kempe 1978; La Fontaine 1990) or between a child and a post-pubescent or sexually mature person (Fritz et al. 1981; Baker and Duncan 1985). In other cases, however, clear age differentials are specified, for example 5 years difference between victim and perpetrator for children under 12, and 8 or 10 years for children over 12 (Finkelhor 1979; Risin and Koss 1987; Fromuth and Burkhart 1989). In other studies a 5 year differential is set but the perpetrator must also be over a certain age, usually 16 (Kinsey et al. 1953; Haugaard and Emery 1989). Definitions which require an age differential are essentially attempting to operationalise a distinction between abusive sexual experiences and cases of sexual exploration among peers, and to be sensitive to the problem of consent and the misuse of authority and trust where young children are concerned.

The relationship between abuser and abused

In their attempts to operationalise definitions of child sexual abuse, and to differentiate types of abusive experience, studies have tended to assume particular categories of relationship between victim and perpetrator. In the main these distinguish between people who are relatives or who belong to the same family (intra-familial abuse, incest etc.) and people who are not related to each other (extra-familial abuse). Although in cases of extra-familial abuse a distinction is usually drawn between perpetrators who are known and those who are not known to the victim, in practice these are often blurred, which can lead to child sexual abuse being conceptualised in terms of intra-familial or "stranger" abuse, whereas finer gradations need to be made (Russell 1984; Kelly et al. 1991). For example, categories of sexual abuse need to take account of inter- as well as cross-generational abuse within families; in cases of extra-familial abuse they also need to allow for the inclusion of peers, family friends, acquaintances, baby sitters, and other people in a position of trust or authority, as well as strangers.

Consent, responsibility and legality

Running through many definitions of child sexual abuse are notions about consent, legality, and the exploitation or abuse of positions of trust and responsibility. For example, a number of studies have attempted to take account of the circumstances and context of experiences by including willingness or alternatively feelings of victimisation on the part of the victim, or the use of coercion on the part of the perpetrator. (Siegal et al. 1987; Finkelhor 1984; Lewis 1985; Wyatt 1985). Against this it can be argued that children have neither the understanding, maturity, nor indeed the power to give or withhold their consent, and that definitions must be operationalised in such a way as to overcome this problem, either through age differentials or particular categories of relationship between victim and perpetrator. In addition to this, some studies have reflected the argument that regardless of the victim's perspective, or of the presence or absence of force, child sexual abuse raises questions about the misuse of positions of authority and responsibility which need to be reflected in the design and operationalisation of prevalence studies (Kelly et al. 1991).

Implications for prevalence rates

The way in which child sexual abuse is conceptualised and defined operationally not only influences the overall design of a study and the nature of the questions asked, but also affects the estimates of prevalence which are produced (Wyatt and Peters 1986a). For example, including peer abuse can increase prevalence rates by up to 9% (Finkelhor 1986); including non-contact as well as contact abuse can raise rates by approximately 16% (Russell 1984; Badgely et al. 1984; Kelly et al. 1991). The effect of introducing consent or perceptions of victimisation as part of a definition is hard to measure, but Kelly et al's study (1991) suggests there may be an impact on prevalence rates.

In the light of these considerations, the feasibility study set out to be as inclusive as possible, and to evaluate the possibility of adopting a *post hoc* rather than an *a priori* approach to the issue of definition. As **Sections 2** and **5** demonstrate, information was collected about *any* experiences of a sexual nature before the age of 16, with comprehensive questioning to ascertain the type of activity engaged in and the frequency of occurrence, together with contextual details concerning age, the nature of the relationship, willingness to participate, the use of pressure or force, and perceptions of the event and subsequent effects. In this way data could be analysed according to a range of different definitions, and comparisons made with other studies.

Context and approach

Apart from the issue of whether and how to operationalise a definition of child sexual abuse, additional questions concern the presentation of the study to the general public, both in terms of introducing the subject matter of the study as a whole, and in terms of the context in which to embed particular questions.

Because of the sensitivity of the subject matter, it could be argued that a more oblique approach is preferable when presenting the study initially, so that response rates are not unduly jeopardised as a result of the subject itself. One way of addressing this issue is to include a few questions on child sexual abuse among a battery of other questions, either in an omnibus or general attitude survey, or as part of a study devoted to a different subject (Baker and

Duncan 1985).[1] Although the advantages of this approach are deemed to be that people will take part and reply because they have not been 'put off' by the subject, or because they are 'caught off guard', there are technical, procedural and ethical problems with this approach. In the first place, if childhood sexual experiences are not presented as part of the agenda of the study it is possible to ask only a few basic questions, rather than to explore in any detail the circumstances and effects of the abuse or to further our understanding of its nature. Secondly, there are ethical issues such as the possibility of raising painful memories without any preparation or forewarning for respondents.

An alternative approach is to present the study in a direct way, but emphasising a number of different aspects of the problem. Examples of this include two of Finkelhor's more recent studies focusing on "child molesting and sexual abuse"[2] and "attitudes to child sexual abuse" respectively. (Finkelhor et al. 1990). The drawback of this approach would seem to be that the bulk of questioning tends to refer to associated issues such as child protection, or public perceptions and definitions of what constitutes child sexual abuse, rather than to people's own experiences. Finally, a number of rather more indirect approaches have also been adopted, which refer to childhood or to sexual experiences rather than to child sexual abuse *per se*. These include for example: "child maltreatment";[3] "the sexual exploitation of women" (Russell 1984); and "family, sexuality and violence" (Kelly et al. 1991).

Because of the sensitivity surrounding the term child sexual abuse, and the lack of consensus over definitions, overt references to "abuse" were ultimately rejected in favour of contexts relating to childhood, sexual experience, and children's knowledge and understanding of sex. **Section 2** discusses a range of approaches which were evaluated during the feasibility study.

In addition to considering the case for or against direct references to child sexual abuse in the initial presentation of the study, it was also necessary to decide how to present the questions which were designed to elicit information about sexually abusive experiences. Again, the feasibility study had to evaluate direct as against indirect approaches, and to assess the number and type of screening questions which might be required. Because of the controversial nature of the subject, the lack of any public or professional consensus over definitions, and the wish to avoid forfeiting information in

---

[1] Other studies which have produced evidence on prevalence without setting out to study child sexual abuse *per se* include, for example, Professor Jean Golding's "Children of the Nineties" cohort study, in which a few questions on unwanted sexual experiences in childhood are included in a broader questionnaire concerning health, home and childhood.

[2] March 1981; Questionnaire kindly provided by Dr Finkelhor, Family Research Laboratory, University of New Hampshire

[3] Questionnaire kindly provided by Dr John Briere, University of Southern California, School of Medicine.

cases where respondents themselves did not consider their experience to be abusive, a series of inclusive and neutral approaches were explored. These are discussed in detail in **Sections 2** and **5**.

Response

Linked to the question of context and approach was the issue of whether or not the public in general would be willing to take part in a study about sexual experiences and childhood, and whether or not particular sub-groups of people would be more or less likely to take part, thereby biasing any estimates of prevalence. Overall response rates for prevalence studies carried out in the United States and Britain are difficult to determine, either because the type of sample precludes computation of a response rate, or because comparability between computations cannot be made. However, a review of a number of American studies suggests response rates of between 50% and 69% (Finkelhor 1986).

Two opposing positions can be argued in relation to the direction of a possible bias in response. Whereas one position maintains that people who have been sexually abused in childhood are *less* likely to take part or to answer particular questions because of trauma or embarrassment, another proposes that survivors of child sexual abuse are *more* likely to take part because they welcome an opportunity to tell their story or to draw attention to the problem as a whole. Evidence from studies in the United States is inconclusive, however, revealing no clear trends in the nature or direction of bias. For example, two studies with relatively low response rates produced very different estimates of prevalence: 11% (for men and women) in Kercher and McShane (1984), compared with 54% (for women) in Russell (1984). **Section 3** documents approaches taken to maximise participation, and reports on response rates achieved at different stages of the pilot study.

Sample

A further issue to be addressed in the feasibility study was that of the design and size of a representative national sample. Because of the sensitive nature of the subject, many of the early prevalence studies of child sexual abuse utilised non-probability samples, often with particularly accessible populations, rather than probability samples of local community or national populations. Non-probability "accessibility" samples have included studies among: college students (Finkelhor 1979; Fritz et al. 1981; Fromuth 1983; Seidner and Calhoun 1984; Risin and Koss 1987; Haugaard and Emery 1989; Briere and Runtz 1988; Kelly et al. 1991); and patients from particular G.P. practices (Landis 1956; Nash and West 1985). Other non-probability studies have been carried out among self-selected members of the general public responding to advertisements or to television or magazine sponsored surveys (Kinsey et al. 1953; Koshal 1986). Although such studies may in some cases have achieved large numbers of respondents, (4,444 in the Kinsey study), the methods of sampling impose limitations on the extent to which generalisations can be made from their findings.

Other kinds of non-probability studies, using quota sampling methods, have been carried out both nationally or in local communities (Bell and Weinberg 1981; Wyatt 1985; Lewis 1985; Baker and Duncan 1985; and Finkelhor et al 1990). Very few studies exist to date which have adopted true probability sampling; these include Russell's (1984) community study, and the national Canadian study conducted by Badgely et al. (1984).

In order to provide prevalence estimates of optimum reliability, to allow for the relatively low base rate for child sexual abuse in the general population, to examine the circumstances and effects of child sexual abuse, and to permit a comparative analysis of different sub-groups, a much larger national random sample would be required than has hitherto been attempted. **Section 4** outlines the issues of design for such a sample, including overall size, age range, and appropriate sampling frame(s).

Questionnaire design

The development and design of a standard and largely pre-coded questionnaire was one of the most important and challenging aspects of the feasibility study. Among prevalence studies to date the diversity of approach and differences in level of detail attempted is considerable. For example, studies range from those with a single general question to elicit reports of child sexual abuse to those with a series of detailed triggers and probes, with the evidence suggesting higher prevalence rates for studies with multiple and specific questioning (Finkelhor 1986).

In the light of this finding, but also because a national survey of child sexual abuse in this country would aim to provide a rich source of data on the nature, circumstances and context of abuse as well as to estimate its prevalence among the adult population, the study was committed to asking a wide range of questions about childhood sexual experiences. Consequently, the feasibility study set out to evaluate alternative approaches to the ordering, context and overall length of the schedule; to question wording and language; and to the level of detail considered appropriate or achievable. Material from unstructured interviews with known survivors, together with an evaluation of approaches and techniques utilised in other studies informed the questionnaire design. **Section 5** outlines the development of a series of modules, designed to take the respondent from general background and classificatory questions, through questions about childhood circumstances and relationships, to more explicit questions about early sexual knowledge and experience.

Mode of administration

A wide variety of modes of administration have been used in prevalence studies to date, including: postal questionnaires, telephone interviews, face to face personal interviews, and self-completion booklets filled out in the presence of an interviewer. Although it may be argued that the anonymity offered by self-completion approaches is more appropriate for studies of sensitive subjects such as child sexual abuse (Kelly et al. 1991a), there is some evidence to suggest that face-to-face interviews conducted by well trained interviewers can achieve a measure of rapport which tends to produce higher estimates of prevalence (Russell 1984; Wyatt 1985, Nash and West 1985).

Other considerations in relation to mode of administration relate to the complexity of the data to be collected; generally speaking, self-completion modes require a simple and straightforward structure, and are not appropriate for more detailed or complex questions. Again, because the national survey would aim to provide data on a range of aspects of child sexual abuse, face-to-face interviews would appear to offer a more flexible way of achieving this. **Section 6** describes the mix of face-to-face and self-completion modes assessed during the feasibility study.

Memory and recall

When conducting a retrospective study among adults about their recollection of childhood events, a number of questions have to be addressed in relation to memory and recall. In this regard, it is important, as Finkelhor (1986) argues, to distinguish between memories that are blocked and inaccessible because of associated emotional trauma; experiences which are partially forgotten but which could be recalled through appropriate and sensitive questioning; events which are remembered but which are construed in terms other than those referred to in a study; and experiences which are remembered but withheld for various reasons. Whereas emotional blocking is a source of under-reporting which is unlikely to be overcome through careful survey design, accessing partially hidden or potentially upsetting and embarrassing memories is something which sensitive questioning can address.

A further consideration regarding the accessibility of memories is the extent to which people can accurately recall both the detail and the feelings associated with childhood experiences rather than simply providing *post hoc* adult reconstructions. There may also be related issues connected with the validity as well as the reliability of adult recall; the so-called 'false memory syndrome'. **Section 7** discusses these issues and describes the strategies adopted in the feasibility study to provide a number of triggers and hooks to facilitate, stimulate and locate childhood memories.

Interviewer preparation and training

If face-to-face interviewing is to be included as a possible mode of administration for a national survey, then careful consideration must be given to the thorough training, preparation and support of interviewers. Evidence from the literature (Russell 1984 Wyatt 1985; Nash and West 1985), and from interviews with survivors, points to the importance of well trained, professional interviewers who are able to establish rapport, whilst remaining entirely neutral and giving no hint of embarrassment, disapproval or judgement. Whilst these qualities are of course required for any survey, a study of child sexual abuse may well call for interviewers to collect information about events which lie outside their own experience, or which arouse disturbing or distressing emotions. **Section 8** outlines the measures taken to prepare and train interviewers for a study of this kind.

In addition to training and preparation, the feasibility study took account of the possible effects of interviewer characteristics on the disclosure of sensitive information, with particular reference to the advantages or disadvantages of matching interviewer and respondent in terms of gender. The study also considered the question of people with a particular or personal interest in the subject of child sexual abuse, such as perpetrators or victims, gaining access to the field force, and the need for screening or other procedures.

Confidentiality and ethics

Finally, in assessing the feasibility of a national survey of child sexual abuse it is essential to address issues of confidentiality and ethics. These are discussed in detail in **Section 9**. Although standard procedures are generally adopted to ensure confidentiality and anonymity for respondents, in the case of a subject as sensitive as child sexual abuse it is necessary to review these and to question whether further precautions and re-assurances are required. For example, it may be necessary to devise additional measures to ensure that certain respondent details cannot be linked to the questionnaires, and to consider providing alternative venues to ensure privacy for the interview itself.

On the question of ethics a number of issues are raised. Primarily these concern the possible effects of the interviews on adult survivors, whereby painful memories may be triggered and traumatic experiences recalled. In the light of this, the feasibility study attempted to identify the extent to which the interviews do indeed cause distress, to evaluate the kind of the post-interview support which could or should be provided, and to establish whether or not the legitimacy and value of a prevalence study are perceived to outweigh its potentially distressing nature.

A further issue in this regard concerns the disclosure of information about third parties, and the possible indication of past or ongoing criminal activity. The need to guarantee confidentiality has therefore to be evaluated relative to the desirability of reporting cases of child sexual abuse.

Each of these technical, methodological and ethical issues is discussed in detail in the following sections of this report. Our conclusions and recommendations in the light of the feasibility study are outlined in **Section 10**.

Section Two

Context and approach

How should the study be presented to the public?

General Issues

The issue of how to approach members of the public, and in what broad context to present a study of child sexual abuse was one of the most fundamental issues of the feasibility study. The need to maximise response is not necessarily compatible with the need to work within ethical boundaries, and much of our work centred on resolution of this dilemma. Previous prevalence studies of child sexual abuse have opted for one of three possible solutions; an oblique approach in which questions about child sexual abuse are embedded within or ended-on to questions about other, largely unrelated topics, a direct approach in which child sexual abuse (usually defined in a given way) is presented as the main topic of the survey, or an indirect approach of one kind or another which nevertheless refers to aspects of sexual experience in childhood. As we have discussed in Section 1, theoretically initial recruitment of respondents to a survey may be easier using oblique methods, since mention of sensitive issues can be avoided when introducing the research. However, although *overall* response may be maximised, there is a cost in terms of lowered *item* response. For example, the MORI survey (Baker and Duncan 1985) which asked questions about sexual abuse in the context of a general survey of young people in Britain had an item refusal rate of 13% for the initial screening question on abusive experiences in childhood. There are also inherent ethical difficulties in obtaining respondents' consent to participate by withholding information, and related technical restrictions in the amount of data that can be collected in this way. Conversely, although direct approaches are clearly ethically and technically preferable if the purpose of the survey is to collect detailed information about child sexual abuse, recruiting respondents to the survey is a much more challenging task when a direct approach is used. Overall response may be dramatically lowered if the initial approach seems too threatening or off-putting. Additionally, although the introduction to the survey must be specific enough to allow people to make informed decisions as to whether or not to participate, it must also be sufficiently wide and *non*-specific to hold saliency for respondents with a range of sexual experience. Finally, the effect that direct approaches have on prevalence rates is unknown. On the one hand, there is the possibility that survivors of child sexual abuse might exclude themselves from studies in which the initial approach indicates that probing questions on abuse will be asked, thus lowering prevalence rates; conversely, those with nothing to report may also exclude themselves because they do not regard the subject of the survey as salient to their own experience, which would have the reverse effect of artificially inflating prevalence figures.

In this section, then, we discuss the various methods of approach which were tested over the course of the study, and report on the advantages and disadvantages of each variant. We begin, however, by discussing the broad context within which approaches were set.

Setting the Study in Context: childhood and the family

From an early point in the study it was apparent to us that the overall context in which we set the research interview would be of paramount importance in conditioning the quality of the data we could collect. Our reading of the literature, and our lengthy and detailed interviews with survivors of child sexual abuse clearly indicated that the context in which abuse occurs is of crucial significance in arriving at an understanding of the phenomenon. Previous research has shown that a large proportion of child sexual abuse occurs within the home and is perpetrated by family members or persons known to the child and to the family rather than consisting only of isolated events perpetrated by strangers (Peters 1976; Finkelhor 1979, 1980; Baker 1983). Moreover, the survivors whom we interviewed in Phase Two of the study emphasised strongly that irrespective of whether the abuse had been perpetrated within or outside the family, to understand what had happened to them we needed detailed information on various aspects of their childhood and upbringing and on their relationships within the family. To build up a complete picture of the abuse, to understand how it had come about and what effects it had led to, it was necessary to probe in some detail the childhood family circumstances of the respondent. Important questions such as how perpetrators gain access to children, how they obtain compliance on the part of the child, and how they maintain secrecy can only be addressed in the context of the child's family and other support networks. Thus it seemed clear that the most appropriate context in which to set the study was that of childhood and the family.[1] Although it was recognised that in choosing childhood as a context we were already entering the realms of the 'sensitive' subject, it appeared that no other context would hold as much scope for investigation of child sexual abuse in all its complexity.

This overall context therefore formed the basis of the different methods of approach which were piloted in the study. One oblique and four more or less direct approaches were tested, and in every phase of the study, at the end of

[1] Because of the focus on early sexual experiences, 16, the age of consent was felt to be more appropriate as an age limit than 18, the age of majority. Thus, "childhood" was defined as the period before the age of 16 for the purposes of the feasibility study.

each interview, we asked respondents to assess the extent to which they felt they had been prepared in advance for the subject and form of the interview by the initial introduction. This was also discussed in some detail in the callback interviews after Phase Four. We drew on these sources of information, as well as feedback from interviewers and data on response in each pre-pilot in order to develop each new approach.

Introducing the Survey: an oblique approach

The first attempt at approaching the general public used an oblique approach, introduced by interviewers as **"a survey of childhood and family life"**[2]. Although interviewers found this an easy approach to make, this initial benefit was offset by the difficulties it created within the actual interview. Making the transition from general childhood-related issues to the subject of childhood sexual experiences felt very awkward given that respondents had not been prepared in advance for these more probing questions. From a technical perspective, the difficulty of making the transition, and the amount of time spent asking about general issues also meant that fewer questions overall could be asked about sexual experiences, thus restricting the breadth of the data collected. The advantages and disadvantages of this approach are summarized below:

Oblique Approach

Subject: **"a national survey of childhood and family life"**

Purpose: "to gain a better understanding of changing patterns of
                     family life and people's experiences during childhood, and
                     to help target resources and plan services for children and
                     young people"

Advantages: — unthreatening, easy to introduce
                     — "services for children" appeals to altruism of respondent

Disadvantages: — title too vague, leaving respondents unsure of what to
                        expect from the interview
                     — emphasis on services for children put off those with no
                        interest in this (e.g. those with no children of their own)
                     — purpose too vague; harder to grasp usefulness of survey
                     — hard to justify extensive questioning on sexual experi-
                        ences
                     — avoidance of mentioning sexual matters ethically
                        questionable

---

[2] Examples of supporting letters given to respondents for each of the five approaches used will be found in the technical appendix.

Introducing the Survey: direct approaches

Our concerns about the serious ethical difficulties of an oblique method of approach within the broad overall context of childhood, and our desire to collect data of more complexity and sophistication than would be possible with only a few questions bedded in a survey about another topic led us to conclude that a direct approach of some form or other was the only viable alternative.

Over the course of the study we experimented with four different forms of more or less direct approach. Each variant had its own strengths and weaknesses, and the challenge was to arrive at a method of introducing the survey to respondents which would be both comprehensive but brief; which would be sufficiently informative to satisfy ethical considerations, but which would not seem threatening and thus discourage people from taking part; and which would be broad enough to seem relevant to all respondents irrespective of their personal history. In the final event, the approach which proved most successful in terms of the need to be both non-threatening and inclusive/ salient, whilst at the same time being ethically satisfactory was approach (d), one which introduced the survey as about **"adults' memories of child-hood, growing up, and learning about sex and sexual development"** (*see below*). This approach was direct in the sense that it explicitly alerted the respondent to the fact that we would ask about childhood experiences in the context of sexual development and sex, but by setting these in the context of normal processes such as "growing up", strove to be as unthreatening and as inclusive as possible. The purpose of the survey was clearly stated, with specific services for children and young people mentioned. The social benefits of participating in the survey were therefore apparent to potential respondents, and interviewers reported that stressing this acted as a incentive to participation for many respondents.

The various approaches that were used and their relative advantages and disadvantages are summarized overleaf:

Direct Approach (a)

Subject: **"a national survey of childhood and children's understanding of sex"**

Purpose: "to gain a better understanding of people's experience during childhood, and to help target resources and plan services for children and young people in areas such as: child health and development, sex education and personal safety for children and young people who may be at risk of unwanted sexual experiences"

Advantages:
— informs respondent of focus on sexual matters
— mentions "unwanted sexual experiences"
— states specific purpose to which data will be put
— "services for children" appeals to altruism of respondent

Disadvantages:
— does not explicitly inform respondent of focus on sexual experiences
— emphasis on services for children put off those with no interest in this (e.g those without children of their own)
— reference to unwanted sexual experiences could limit reporting of wanted experiences

Direct Approach (b)

Subject: **"a national survey of childhood and children's understanding and knowledge of sex"**

Purpose: "to gain a better understanding of people's experience during childhood, and to help target resources and plan services for children and young people in areas such as: child health and development, sex education and personal safety for children and young people who may be at risk of unwanted sexual experiences"

Advantages:
— informs respondent of focus on sexual matters
— includes implied reference to sexual experience ("knowledge" of sex)
— mentions "unwanted sexual experiences"
— states specific purpose to which data will be put
— "services for children" appeals to altruism of respondent

Disadvantages:
— reference to sexual experiences implicit rather than explicit
— emphasis on services for children put off those with no interest in this (e.g those without children of their own)
— reference to unwanted sexual experiences could limit reporting of wanted experiences

Direct Approach (c)

Subject: **"a national survey of public attitudes to child sexual abuse"**

Purpose: "to gain a better understanding of people's experience during childhood, and to help target resources and plan services for children and young people in areas such as: child health and development, sex education and personal safety for children and young people who may be at risk of unwanted sexual experiences"

Advantages: — direct reference to child sexual abuse
                     — topical issue of social concern is incentive to participate
                     — states specific purpose to which data will be put
                     — "services for children" appeals to altruism of respondent

Disadvantages: — emphasis on services for children put off those with no interest in this (e.g those without children of their own)
                     — reference to unwanted sexual experiences could limit reporting of wanted experiences
                     — direct mention of child sexual abuse could be threatening, especially to survivors
                     — runs risk of appealing to "moral majority"
                     — requires substantial questioning on attitudes before subject of own experiences can be raised; limits data collection possibilities
                     — those with no opinions/no interest more likely to refuse

Direct Approach (d): Our selected approach

Subject: **"learning about sex: adults' memories of their own childhood, growing up and what they learned about sexual development and sex, and their views about their own childhood experiences"**

Purpose: "to gain a better understanding of people's experience during childhood, and to help target resources and plan services for children and young people in areas such as: child health and development, sex education and personal safety for children and young people who may be at risk of unwanted sexual experiences"

Advantages: — explicit reference to early sexual experiences
                    — interesting and salient topic to most people
                    — unthreatening; sets study in normative context of growing up

Disadvantages: — emphasis on services for children put off those with no interest in this (e.g those without children of their own)
                    — direct reference to early sexual experiences could be off-putting, especially to survivors
                    — reference to unwanted sexual experiences could limit reporting of wanted experiences

The Direct Approach: maximising participation

As we have already indicated, the decision to adopt a direct approach to recruiting respondents to the survey carries with it certain costs in terms of the extra effort which has to be made to maximise response. In particular, the interviewer's role assumes great significance, since she or he must be highly skilled at overcoming respondents' anxieties about potential embarrassment, in communicating clearly the purpose of the survey and the principle of confidentiality, and in fact in building rapport with a potential respondent from the moment the front door is opened. All of these skills are important tools in interviewing generally, irrespective of the subject of a survey, but in a 'sensitive' survey they become indispensable.

We found that even though all the interviewers who worked in the survey were already extremely experienced and skilled at their job, their performance in terms of achieving a good response improved over the course of the four pre-pilots, (see Section 3). Over the course of the feasibility study certain issues emerged as having a particularly significant bearing on the recruitment process, and we were able to compile the following list of points which interviewers needed to be able to convey clearly and confidently to potential respondents in view of the subject matter of the survey in order to maximise response. Of course many of these points apply to research in general, not just research on a sensitive issue; neither is the list exhaustive, as there are many aspects of initial approach to respondents which can have a bearing on response; however, our findings indicated that these five points required particular attention when designing a strategy for approaching respondents in a survey of this kind:

1. The sample had been selected at random: always an important point to stress, but particularly so from the point of view of survivors of child sexual abuse, who may otherwise feel that they have been specifically targeted for the survey because something is known of their personal history, and may feel deeply threatened by this. (Clinicians also suggested that perpetrators who were included in the sample would also be very likely to suspect they had been specially selected for much the same reasons.)

2. The interviews would be informal and non-threatening: we found that people's worries about the nature of the questions (would they be embarrassing, would they be forced to reveal details they would rather keep private and so forth) were most prominent at this stage of the survey, before the interview had commenced. Reassurance that this would not be the case was therefore very important when introducing the survey.[3]

3. The interviews would be totally confidential: perhaps the most fundamental point of all. Survivors and non-survivors alike stressed this in depth interviews, and interviewers need to be able to give a coherent and authoritative account of the procedures by which confidentiality is maintained by the survey organization.[4]

4. The survey is important, has salience for the respondent, and will provide useful information for a specific purpose: potential respondents need to be convinced that the survey will provide data which is actually needed, and that the research is not simply an exercise in voyeurism or an opportunity to probe into the intimate details of respondents' private lives.

---

[3] In fact, once the interview had started, most respondents discovered their fears in this respect to be unfounded. Many commented after the interview that they had not been as embarrassed or inhibited as they had expected, and had felt able to be very frank with the interviewer.

[4] We also found some evidence from callback interviews that some respondents would benefit from a post-interview confirmation of confidentiality, given the highly personal nature of the information requested by the interviewer. We therefore recommend that some procedure be adopted as routine to accommodate this; for example, a follow-up letter from the survey organization and sponsor re-iterating the purpose of the survey and guaranteeing confidentiality; see Section 10.

Information about the survey, either in letter form or offered by the interviewer, needs to stress the importance of the topic and indicate in concrete terms the use to which this new knowledge will be put; it also needs to convince respondents that the subject is salient to them, even though they may be many years from childhood, or may consider themselves never to have had any early experiences that immediately spring to mind as 'sexual'.

5. **The survey offers the respondent an opportunity to have a voice about an important, topical issue**: it must also be communicated to respondents that careful thought has to be given to the important issue of what they themselves can expect to gain from taking part. This is particularly an issue for survivors, who may take part in the survey at considerable cost to themselves in terms of reviving traumatic memories and revealing very personal information, and perhaps even putting themselves at risk of retaliatory action by perpetrators. We found that despite this, survivors appreciated the opportunity to tell their story and express their views, and that stressing this opportunity could be a powerful incentive to take part.

Response and response bias

Will people take part in a survey of childhood sexual experiences?

In this section we discuss issues relating to response[1] to the feasibility study, and consider sources of potential bias. The implications of findings on each of these are assessed, and strategies for maximising response and minimising bias in a national survey are suggested. It must be stressed that because of the comparatively low base rate of child sexual abuse (and particularly certain forms of abuse) a full scale pilot would be necessary to investigate response more thoroughly; (see Section 4). Furthermore, because the sample sizes in each of the four pre-pilots were small, only tentative conclusions regarding response or response bias can be drawn. It should be remembered that the method of sampling varied between pre-pilots, as did our strategy for approaching respondents, and thus caution must be exercised in generalizing from the overall results. Our comments here should therefore be taken as indications only of likely trends in response and bias, which we see as providing a basis for further investigation by means of a larger pilot or pilots.

The outcome figures for each of the four pre-pilots are given in detail in the Technical Appendix. Quota samples were used in the first two pre-pilots, and because of the non-random nature of such samples (Moser and Kalton 1971), we limit ourselves to qualitative observations on response for these. In pre-pilots 3 and 4, however, random samples were used (within a given geographical area) and we are able to gain some firmer indications as to the likely shape of response in terms of which groups would be over or under-represented in such a survey, and what steps might be necessary to ensure good coverage of the population.

Overall Response

Our findings indicated that people will undoubtedly take part in a survey of this kind, and overall response rates were encouraging. The results from pre-pilots 3 and 4 are shown in Table 3.2 below. Although the response rate in pre-pilot 3[2], calculated as a proportion of addresses known to be in

---

[1] It should be noted that this section deals only with overall response, and not item response, which is discussed in Section 5.

[2] Because we carried out a split run using two different approaches and questionnaires in pre-pilot 3, the figures given here refer only to the results of the approach used to generate the bulk of the interviews. This was approach "b", which introduced the survey as "a national survey of childhood and children's knowledge and understanding of sex". (See Section 2 for further details).

scope[3] was 56%, somewhat lower than would normally be expected in a national survey, given the short fieldwork period allowed (one week) and the sensitivity of the subject matter, we were not too discouraged by this. In pre-pilot 4, we were able to raise the response rate to 71%, again, with only a short fieldwork period allowed. This rise in response was probably due to a number of factors, including improved approach technique, better respondent information materials, and increased interviewer confidence and familiarity with the survey (see below). This figure is most encouraging, and is in line with the recent survey of sexual attitudes and lifestyles in which a response rate of 71.5% was achieved among in scope households where an eligible respondent could be identified and selected, (Johnson et al 1992).[4] It also compares well with the few other studies of child sexual abuse using random sampling methods; for example, Russell's (1984) study of women in San Francisco, in which she reports a response rate of 64%.

Table 3.1 **Outcome in pre-pilots 3 and 4: summary data**

	Pre-pilot 3*	Pre-pilot 4
Issued	113	175
Out of scope (Ineligibles, unavailable during fieldwork period**, non-contacts, deadwood, unused	61	107
In scope:	52	68
Refusals	23 (44%)	20 (29%)
Productive interviews	29 (56%)	48 (71%)

 * Approach "b" only
** Because of the very short fieldwork period, respondents who were temporarily unavailable for interview during this time were included in the out of scope category. There remains, of course, the possibility that with longer fieldwork periods and continuing unavailability, some of these people should have been recoded to the in scope/refusal category.

In terms of area, as Table 3.2 shows, the number of productive interviews did not appear to vary a great deal from one area to the next. Although surveys in general tend to show poorer response rates in London and the South East, response in these areas was only slightly lower than elsewhere. Nevertheless, evidence from the National Survey of Sexual Attitudes and

---

[3] We calculate response here as a proportion of addresses known to be in scope; that is, as a proportion of households where an eligible respondent could be identified and selected. In both pre-pilots, partly due to the short fieldwork periods, a relatively large number of addresses were classified as out of scope; see Technical Appendix for details.

[4] Our results compare particularly favourably with these figures as the rate for the National survey excludes households where a complete refusal of information was encountered, whereas our figures include these with other refusals.

Lifestyles suggests that in a large scale survey on a sensitive issue, one should be prepared for lower response in the London area; in that survey the response rate in London was almost 10% below the national average.

Table 3.2 **Productive Interviews by area – pre-pilots 3 and 4 combined**

Area	Productive interviews	(Total Issued)
Bradford	19	(44)
Birmingham	15	(43)
Reading	19	(44)
Portsmouth	15	(44)
Essex	15	(44)
London	16	(44)
Newcastle*	5	(25)
All	77	(288)

*Pre-pilot 4 only.

Our results also confirm that it is possible to obtain interviews with a good cross-section of the population in terms of demographic characteristics; over the course of the four pre-pilots we achieved 127 productive interviews, and as Table 3.3 shows, both men and women from a range of age groups and occupational classes took part in the survey.

Table 3.3 **Productive interviews by sex, age and occupation***

		PRE-PILOT				
		(Quota sample)		(Random sample)		
		1	2	3	4	All
Productive interviews		21	20	38	48	127
Sex	Male	9	10	18	21	58
	Female	12	10	20	27	69
Age	18–25	3	4	2	8	17
	26–35	9	6	17	11	43
	36–45	3	5	10	14	31
	46–60	6	5	9	15	34
Occupation	Manual	10	6	13	16	45
	Non-manual	7	13	23	23	66
	Other (not working)	4	1	2	9	16

*Main wage-earner in household

Is there any bias in response?

Although the feasibility study was not intended to provide data comparable with general population data, examination of the characteristics of respondents tentatively suggests that some sections of the population may have been somewhat under-represented. Males, young people and those in manual occupations may be less likely to take part in a survey of this kind. Although we stress that small sample sizes mean this may reflect random sampling variation rather than systematic bias in response, some evidence from the recent survey on sexual matters suggests that in particular, the finding in relation to gender may be a typical form of bias in surveys on sensitive issues. For example, the National Survey of Sexual Attitudes and Lifestyles carried out for the Wellcome Trust found a tendency for non-responders to be male (Johnson et al. 1992). Since the present study was concerned with sexual matters in childhood, an even more taboo subject than sexual matters in adulthood, we were not surprised to find this pattern emerging again. Clearly, a large scale pilot should investigate this further, and incorporate measures to encourage response from these more difficult-to-recruit groups.[5]

Will people who have had sexual experiences[6] in childhood take part?

Again, our findings on participation in the survey by those who had had sexual experiences before the age of 16 were encouraging. Respondents reported a range of experiences, both positive and negative in character. These varied from sexual games and exploration with peers and siblings such as playing 'doctors and nurses' and consensual childhood and teenage sexual relationships, to experiences with both peers and adults which were rated as non-consensual and traumatic, many of which would certainly fall into research definitions of sexual abuse.[7] The fact that respondents felt able to disclose sexual experiences of this most sensitive nature gives us confidence that it is possible, in a survey of this kind, to pick up a very wide range of experiences, including those which are broadly representative of the phenomenon of sexual abuse as documented in the clinical literature as well as other more normative sexual experiences. Respondents were asked to describe up to four experiences, and although only one respondent reported four, many reported two or three experiences before 16.

[5] Additionally, because of small sample sizes, we were not able to reach any conclusions regarding other possible sources of bias; for example, those related to religious or ethnic identity. Again, a large scale pilot would provide the opportunity to investigate these issues further.

[6] We define a sexual 'experience' here as a single event involving at least one other person, or as a series of events involving the same other person or group of persons.

[7] Theoretical and operational considerations in the concept of "willingness" are discussed in Section 5.

Wanted or 'willing' experiences

Across the four pre-pilots, 54 respondents (43%) reported 67 childhood sexual experiences in which they described themselves as willing or indifferent participants. Respondents ranged in age from 4 years to 15 years old at the time of these experiences, and the vast majority were with same age peers or other children or young people of not more than 2 years age difference. One notable exception was a prolonged series of sexual contacts reported by a male respondent between himself as a 12 year old with a 27 year old woman. The range of experiences reported was wide, from sexual games such as 'doctors and nurses' and mutual exploration of genitalia between young children, through to adolescent sexual experimentation including regular sexual intercourse. Both same-sex and heterosexual experiences were reported.

Unwanted or 'unwilling' experiences

Over the four pre-pilots, a total of 46 unwanted sexual experiences were reported by 36 respondents composed of 25 women and 11 men. Half (23 experiences) did not involve actual physical contact with the child (such as indecent exposure or "flashing") and half concerned sexual activities involving physical contact ranging from unwanted fondling to violent sexual assault and battery. 33 incidents were described by female respondents and 13 were described by male respondents. All but one experience involved exclusive perpetration by a male or males, and 42 of the 46 experiences were single or "one off" incidents whilst 4 were experiences involving two or more sexual contacts with the same perpetrator (for example, sexual contact with a step father over many years). Table 3.4 summarizes the unwanted experiences reported by respondents.

Table 3.4   **Unwanted sexual experiences before the age of 16: summary data – Pre-pilots 1–4**

Base = All unwanted experiences*	
Genital fondling/masturbation	13
Intercourse	2
Rape/attempted rape	6
Non-genital fondling	2
Sexual talk/suggestions/invitations	5
Indecent exposure/flashing	18
Total number of contact experiences	23
Total number of non-contact experiences	23
All unwanted experiences	46

*Reported by 36 respondents

Respondent ages at first sexual contact, and the ages of the perpetrators involved (as estimated by respondents) are given in Tables 3.5 and 3.6. Respondents ranged in age from five to fifteen years, and perpetrators ranged from ten years old to an estimated late 50s.

Table 3.5 **Respondent ages at first sexual contact: unwanted experiences**

Base = All unwanted experiences

Age in years	Number of cases
Under 7	3
7 to 11	13
12 to 15	28
Unclear	2
All	46

Table 3.6 **Perpetrator ages* at first sexual contact: unwanted experiences**

Base = All unwanted experiences

Age in years	Number of cases
10 to 15	3
16 to 21	9
22 to 30	9
31 to 40	10
Over 40	8
Unclear/unknown	7
All	46

*Ages are estimated in some cases

The relationship of perpetrators to respondents is given in Table 3.7. As would be expected from the relatively large proportion of indecent exposures reported by the sample as a whole, well over half of all unwanted sexual experiences involved strangers.

Table 3.7 **Relationship of perpetrators to respondents: unwanted experiences**

Base = All unwanted experiences

Relationship of perpetrator to respondent	Number of cases
Peer	5
Acquaintance/known by sight	4
Authority figure	3
Neighbour, family friend	4
Relative	2
Stranger	28
All	46

The purpose of the feasibility study was not, of course, to produce reliable data on childhood sexual experiences and the sample sizes involved render it inappropriate to make generalisations based on the number or range of experiences reported. The small numbers involved in this study and widely differing methodologies in other studies mean comparisons can only be made in a very broad sense. However, these results (28% of the four samples combined reporting unwanted sexual experiences, or 36% of women and 18% of men), appear to be well within the range of prevalence rates found in large scale studies of child sexual abuse carried out in Britain and North America, (see Section 1).

It is also of interest to note the range of incidents that were reported, including a comparatively large proportion of non-contact and stranger-perpetrated incidents such as flashing, relative to some other studies. For example, Russell (1984) found only 15% and Finkelhor (1979) found only 27% of unwanted sexual experiences involved strangers. Differences in definitions and methodologies used in other studies, and differing styles of presentation of results make direct comparisons impossible to achieve, but our findings indicate the merits of an approach which avoids pre-definition of sexual experiences. For example, our research suggested that being subjected to indecent exposure is a common experience in childhood, but the extent to which such an experience is perceived as coercive or victimising was found to depend to a large extent on the circumstances surrounding the event. An incident occurring at dusk or after dark, or where the child was alone at the time or in a place they knew to be 'out of bounds' might be perceived as extremely frightening and threatening by the respondent. Equally, the same incident occurring in daylight hours or in the company of other children might be regarded as trivial. Adult attributions may also play a role; we found a tendency for intervening adult rationalisations to dismiss certain sorts of incidents as insignificant 'in retrospect', thus obscuring childhood percep-tions of the event at the time. Because of these factors, in the interests of maximising item response in terms of the reporting of the whole range of childhood sexual experiences of respondents, our research confirms the importance of removing the 'negative' emphasis from operational definitions used in prevalence research (although we stress this should not be taken as meaning the same applies to theoretical or analytic definitions, for which negative perceptions may be highly salient). If we had asked, as did Russell (1984) whether respondents had ever "been upset" by an indecent exposure; or if we had asked questions in the context of coercive or unwanted experiences, chances are that without further probing many of these sorts of incidents would not have been reported. We attach particular importance to this point because of the need to clarify conceptual issues in the definition of child sexual abuse. We believe that it is vital that research in this area should develop methodologies which can capture the whole range of childhood sexual experiences, together with sufficient information to determine the significance of different types of event in terms of their perception by, and effects on, the respondent. Only then will it be possible to address the question of what should and should not be considered as 'child sexual abuse'.[8]

What are the reasons for non-response?

We made strenuous efforts to gain as much information about non-respondents as possible in terms of their reasons for refusal to take part. Interviewers were instructed to probe for reasons for refusal in as much detail as they were able, and failing a clear answer, to ask specifically whether the subject of the survey was felt to be off-putting. Additionally, after pre-pilot 3 we mailed a short questionnaire to all non-responding households or individuals in which we solicited information about reasons for refusal, and received replies back from nearly half of those who had refused[9]. Although it was not always possible to establish a definitive reason for refusal, our tentative conclusions were that a relatively small proportion of non-response was due to the specific subject of the survey. Most people who gave an answer gave general reasons for refusal to participate – for example not approving of surveys, being too busy or pre-occupied with personal matters, or just lack of interest[10]. Some people (especially in earlier pre-pilots, before interviewers had become familiar with strategies for overcoming such objections) failed to see the salience to themselves or the importance generally of the survey subject and refused on these grounds.

Nevertheless, examination of Address Record Forms[11] and 'refusers' questionnaires in pre-pilots 3 and 4 indicated that a proportion of non-respondents across the four pre-pilots did refuse to take part because of the subject matter of the survey. Some reasons appeared to be related to the general belief that matters connected with sexual experience are too private to be discussed with an interviewer, for example, one person commented: "I don't discuss my private life with strangers." However, other people clearly had specific experiences which they wished to keep private, although the

---

[8] An alternative interpretation of our finding that a relatively large proportion of experiences are extra-familial or stranger-perpetrated could of course be that *intra*-familial or non-stranger experiences were under-reported. We think this is unlikely, however. Rather, our findings probably reflect the propensity of previous studies to under-estimate the incidence of stranger-perpetrated sexual encounters, due to differences of definition and approach, as discussed above.

[9] A copy of the non-respondent's questionnaire is included in the Technical Appendix.

[10] These general reasons could, of course, conceal more specific reasons for non-participation. However, we are guided in our conclusions by interviewers' assessments after their considerable efforts to probe reasons fully.

[11] Address Record Forms are the documents on which interviewers record the details of their contact at a particular address or household, including reasons for non-participation by a selected individual.

reasons given tended to be vague (for example, one person told an interviewer their childhood was "awful beyond belief" and they did not want to
remember any of it, and another refusal was received because of "very
personal and private reasons to do with the subject of the survey"). Evidence
of this kind, coupled with anecdotal evidence from interviewer reports of
some non-respondent reactions on being approached to take part in the
survey (uncertainty, distress, or hostility for example) led us to speculate that
these reactions may be related to traumatic experiences, although we cannot,
of course, reach any firm conclusions on this matter. Table 3.8 summarizes
the reasons for refusal received in pre-pilots 3 and 4.

Table 3.8 **Reasons given by non-respondents for refusal:
pre-pilots 3 and 4**

Base = All refusals	
Objected to subject	9
No interest in subject	4
Other reasons	14
Unclear/not stated	16
All	43

Conclusions: Implications for response, and strategies for minimising bias

Our findings on overall response to the four pre-pilots were most encouraging, with response rates up to 71% by the final pre-pilot. This is very good
level of response for a survey on a sensitive issue; furthermore it compares
favourably with other studies on sexual experience (both childhood and
adult), being as high or in many cases higher than the response rates achieved
in other surveys. Although small numbers indicate caution, the prevalence
estimates suggested by our study are well within the range of estimates
produced by other studies. We are also confident that a good cross-section of
the population with a variety of sexual histories, including those who have
had experiences which would be classified as abusive, can be encouraged to
take part in a survey of this kind.

There are some indications, however, that in terms of overall response, a
survey of this kind may be subject to some degree of bias, both in terms of the
demographic characteristics of the sample and in terms of the sexual history
of respondents. Only a full-scale pilot would reveal whether these effects are
of a significant order. There are also some suggestions that the culturally
taboo nature of the subject may discourage some people from participating,
either because they regard sexual experience in childhood as an essentially
private subject, or because they themselves have had experiences which they
would prefer not to reveal to an interviewer. We further suspect that this may

be particularly the case where the experiences in question have been traumatic or abusive. However, since some refusals will also be due to lack of interest in the study by those who have *not* had any memorable sexual experiences in childhood, this bias may be offset to a certain extent. Although these potential biases should be acknowledged, we do not think they constitute a fundamental threat to the reliability or validity of a national survey. Although some respondents with painful childhood memories may decline to participate, as our results show, many respondents of this kind *can* be encouraged to take part, given the right method of approach. Furthermore, we feel that attention to rigorous fieldwork procedures can go a long way towards maximising response and minimising bias. On the basis of our experience over the course of the feasibility study, we therefore recommend the following procedures should be undertaken in a full-scale survey:

1 Re-issue refusals to alternative interviewers. This was highly successful in boosting response rates in the recent National Survey of Sexual Attitudes and Lifestyles; there is evidence that with sensitive subjects a more experienced interviewer (or simply a different interviewer) can often persuade a "borderline" non-respondent to convert. For example, in the aforementioned survey, 23% of initial refusals were converted to productive interviews by re-issuing.[12] Re-issues demonstrate a high level of commitment to the survey by the survey organization and sponsoring body, and serve to raise the respondent's evaluation of the importance of the survey. They can also be successful in overcoming refusals related to interviewer characteristics; for example, it may be that the gender of the interviewer prompted a refusal because of the subject of the survey. Offering an interviewer of the preferred gender may overcome the respondent's objections. The corollary of this is that longer than average fieldwork periods would need to be budgeted for.

2 Undertake thorough interviewer training in approach techniques. Interviewers who have been thoroughly briefed on good approach techniques, and trained to be sensitive to the likely reactions of different groups in the population will achieve better response rates than those who have not. Although we discuss interviewer training in more detail in section 8, it is worth noting here that we consider interviewer skills to be a vital component of a high response rate in a survey on this subject. For this reason, we do not think it desirable that a large number of new or inexperienced interviewers be used in survey of this kind, although practical considerations (such as large sample size; see Section 4) may make this ideal more difficult to achieve.

---

[12] Re-issuing is also used to good effect on non-sensitive but "hard to sell" surveys such as the British Social Attitudes Survey series which SCPR carries out every year.

3   Provide high-quality literature for respondents to support interviewers' explanations. Feedback from respondents and information from the callback interviews indicated that the quality of the explanatory letter given to respondents made a difference to how respondents perceived the study. Over the course of the four pre-pilots we modified our letter to respondents considerably, not just to reflect changes in content as we experimented with different approaches, but also in design and layout. The letter which was most favourably received and which we used in the final pilot was extremely concise, in a question-and-answer format (see Technical Appendix), and reproduced on high quality paper headed with both Department of Health and SCPR logos, signed by SCPR researchers and a representative of the Department. Respondents apparently felt more reassured by a well-produced letter as to the bona fide nature of the survey, and we found that the question-and-answer format seemed to provide the most digestible way of presenting the information, so that having read the letter, fewer respondents claimed still to be unsure of what to expect from the survey. Although this would have to be investigated more fully in a larger-scale pilot, we also have reason to suspect that sending letters in advance was not, in this particular survey, an advantage. Our impression was that owing to the sensitive, possibly controversial subject of the survey, letters sent in advance were prone to become the subject of family discussions which were not conducive to high response rates. Specifically, we found that non-responders appeared to have been adversely influenced by the negative reactions of other members of the household, and would cite other peoples' views as a reason for refusing, for example: "I wouldn't have minded taking part, but my husband/wife/parent thinks I shouldn't."[13]

Finally, we also feel that although there may be groups who will be less likely to participate in the survey than others, it may be possible to quantify this type of bias to some extent. For example, following up non-responders with a short questionnaire may enable evaluation of reasons for refusals. There are, however, ethical issues to be considered here, such as the extent to which it is appropriate to pursue someone who may have a painful personal history which they do not wish to discuss.

---

[13] This is of course an artefact of the sampling method, in that samples not consisting of named respondents but of households from which a selection is made (such as we propose here: see Technical Appendix for details), make it inevitable that the letter is available to non-sample members as well as sample members.

Sampling

In this section we discuss the theoretical and technical issues connected with defining the limits of the sample, suggest appropriate sampling frames and sampling procedures, and estimate differing sample sizes which should be achieved given the varying base rates of child sexual abuse estimated by previous prevalence studies.

Clearly, before sample design can be addressed, it is necessary to identify which groups in the population are to be included in the survey. Issues such as lower and upper age limits, cultural background, and whether those in institutions are to be included need to be resolved.

Defining the Population Under Study

Lower Age Limits

Because of various considerations, we fixed a lower age limit of 18 years for inclusion in any of the four pre-pilots. One very important reason for this decision was that we felt prevalence rates for those under eighteen would be highly unreliable, since below this age, parental agreement, if not signed consent, might have to be sought before an interview was carried out. In view of the fact that a substantial proportion of child sexual abuse is perpetrated by parents, guardians or other family members this is obviously undesirable. Seeking parental approval for interviews would introduce bias, in that parents or guardians of young people known or suspected to have been abused would be unlikely to consent to the interview for fear of the consequences of disclosure. Equally they might insist on being present at the interview in order to monitor what was said, thus inhibiting the young person from answering frankly. Parents may also refuse on behalf of the young person if they deem the subject of the survey inappropriate or irrelevant. For example, parents may feel they are more knowledgable about the content of their child's personal or sexual experience than they actually are, and may refuse because they (erroneously) believe the young person has no relevant experience of sexual matters. Either way, we feel both overall response rates and item response rates for this age group would be crucially reduced by having to seek parental co-operation or agreement for an interview.

Perhaps even more importantly, there are grave ethical difficulties in conducting interviews of this kind with young people. It could be argued that young people who may not have had extensive sexual experience themselves are not appropriate subjects for a survey which includes probing questions about sexual activity. An even more fundamental problem is, however, that most young people under eighteen are still resident in the parental home, and those who have been sexually abused within the home may reside with a perpetrator, particularly if the abuse has remained undisclosed. Furthermore, young people for whom abuse is a recent or current issue might be severely traumatised by being asked to take part in a survey of this kind. For these reasons we feel the emotional and physical wellbeing of this most vulnerable group of young people could be severely compromised by an approach to take part in a survey of childhood sexual experience. The ethical implications of this are further discussed in Section 9.

In fact, although technically the problem of parental agreement does not exist if only those aged 18 and above are included in the survey, some of the other problems listed above do continue to apply to other young adults aged 18 or over. In the four pre-pilots we found that of respondents 25 and under, more were still living in the parental home than were not, and that this could create problems of privacy for the respondent. Parents continued to act as gatekeepers to this age group; some proxy refusals were received because of this, with the interviewer being denied access to the potential respondent to seek first hand information.[1] Given the subject of the survey, we raise for consideration the suggestion that a higher than usual minimum age might be more appropriate; perhaps 20 or even 25 instead of the more usual 18.

Upper Age Limits

The issue of upper age limit is less vexed than that of lower age limits. We set an upper limit of 60 years of age for each of the four pre-pilots; and although it has sometimes been suggested that more elderly people might be offended by the subject matter of a survey such as this one[2], we found this not to be the case. In fact older people tended to be very positive about the likely value of the survey to present day and future children. Indeed, interviewers commented that many people who were approached but then found to be over 60 years of age were most disappointed not to be able to take part in the survey. There are of course problems of recall as respondents further and further away from childhood are included in the sample; even though long-term memory is thought to be less affected by ageing than short-term memory, the fine detail of recall may be less reliable with this older age group. The great advantage, however, of including as wide a range of ages as possible is that patterns of childhood experience over time can be studied and

---

[1] For example, one mother and father refused point blank to allow the interviewer to approach their daughter on "personal" grounds and even phoned SCPR's offices to insist that no further approaches should be made after the interviewer had left.

[2] For example, the National Survey of Sexual Attitudes and Lifestyles found older people less likely to respond than younger people. (Johnson et al. 1992).

compared, providing data to address the question of whether the incidence of child sexual abuse has been increasing or decreasing over time, thus setting current debates about child sexual abuse in historical context. Diana Russell's (1984) study of women in San Francisco provided interesting data on this for America suggesting that rates of extra-familial child victimisation had remained fairly stable over time while rates of intra-familial abuse have fluctuated; British data has yet to be provided on this subject, and a national survey would provide an excellent opportunity to fill this gap in the knowledge base.

Cultural Background

Another issue which has to be addressed is that of the cultural background of respondents. For example, to what extent are data pertaining to childhood in other cultures comparable with those pertaining to childhood in Britain? How much variation in behaviours towards children are to be found amongst the different cultural groups within Britain itself? We made it a criterion for eligibility in the pre-pilot surveys that respondents should have had their main residence in Britain by the age of four in order that questions on schooling, family organization, patterns of caretaking and access to sexual education were presented in broadly the same cultural context; however, if the purpose of the survey is to investigate the numbers of adults in Britain who have been sexually victimised irrespective of whether the victimisation happened in Britain or elsewhere, a more cross-cultural approach would need to be adopted. Additionally, adults not brought up in Britain are less likely than others to have sufficient English to carry out a standard interview, and the implications for confidentiality of using proxy respondents or interpreters when discussing sensitive subjects would have to be considered carefully. Finally, our small sample sizes meant we had few respondents brought up in Britain but of ethnic minority origin, and relatively few respondents of minority religions. We recognize that allowance for cultural variations in child rearing would need to be built into the questionnaire in more detail than was possible in the feasibility study, and a larger pilot would be needed to investigate the issues surrounding the carrying out of such a survey with respondents from cultural or religious backgrounds in which sexual matters are highly tabooed.

Institutional and Other Special Populations

Certain groups of people, for example long-term residents of psychiatric and other hospitals, prisoners, and the homeless are often routinely excluded from general population surveys because of the practical difficulties inherent in sampling, contacting and obtaining interviews with them. Where the subject of the survey is particularly salient to these populations, additional research effort has to be applied to overcoming these difficulties[3].

This would certainly seem to apply to a survey on the prevalence of child sexual abuse, as there is a large amount of clinical evidence to suggest a link between the experience of certain forms of sexual victimisation in childhood and subsequent deviant status in adulthood. Clinical studies have consistently demonstrated an association between histories of childhood sexual abuse and problems in later adult social, behavioral and emotional functioning, including high levels of psychiatric morbidity, drug abuse, prostitution, delinquency and criminality, homelessness, marital and sexual problems. (Briere and Runtz 1988; Friedrich et al. 1986; Groth and Burgess 1979; Conte 1985, Browne and Finkelhor 1986, and Bolton et al. 1989 for reviews of the literature). Additionally, recent reviews of the research have also highlighted the possibility that children with disabilities may be at increased risk for abuse, and that abuse may be implicated in the creation of disability (Degener 1992, Kelly 1992). Given these data, it seems likely that many people resident in hospitals and other institutions, and many homeless people will be found to have histories involving child sexual abuse. It follows, therefore, that failure to include such people in a national survey will have the effect of producing artificially low prevalence estimates of child sexual abuse overall; in particular, we might hypothesize that many of the most extreme or severe cases of child sexual abuse would not be represented by the survey, since it may be that these cases are most likely to be associated with outcomes such as homelessness, entry into drug abuse or prostitution, or institutionalisation for psychiatric or criminal reasons. Thus to produce an estimate of prevalence which is as close to the true rate as possible it would be desirable to make every effort to include these people in the sample. If inclusion in the main survey proved impossible, we would recommend a special survey be undertaken amongst these groups, replicating as far as possible the methodology used in the main general population survey. The general population data would then provide baseline figures against which to compare results.

Sampling Frames

General Population

Contemporary social research amongst the general population in Britain tends to be carried out using one of two of the most reliable sampling frames; the Electoral Register (ER) or the Postcodes Address File (PAF). The ER is a list of all those eligible to vote in the United Kingdom within the life of the

---

[3] For example, a survey currently being carried out by the Office of Population Censuses and Surveys on psychiatric morbidity includes a sample of people in institutions and homeless people.

register, listed by name and home address. PAF is a quarterly updated, comprehensive list of all the delivery points to which the Post Office delivers mail, and is divided into a mainly residential or small users File (addresses to which an average of 50 or less items of mail per day are delivered) and a non-domestic or large users File (addresses receiving more than 50 items per day on average). The relative merits of these two frames for carrying out probability sampling have been discussed at length elsewhere (e.g Lynn and Lievesley 1991) and need not be rehearsed in detail here. Although the ER has the advantage of yielding a sample of named individuals from different households (and can be drawn to account for differing selection probabilities due to varying household size), doubts about the coverage of the frame, particularly as regards young people, highly mobile people, those in inner cities, non-Commonwealth and New Commonwealth citizens have led researchers away from using the ER in recent years. Our recommendation would therefore be to use the small user PAF for drawing a sample of addresses since this is thought to give superior coverage and is therefore the more reliable sampling frame in this respect[4]. Interviewers would then randomly select individuals within addresses using a random number grid system. This system was used successfully in the last two pre-pilots which were carried out (see Technical Appendix for details), and we feel that this is the technically and theoretically most desirable method of sampling, providing interviewers are suitably trained in making the random selection of respondents.[5]

Institutional and Special Populations

A deficiency shared by both PAF and the ER is that many of those in institutions, and those who have no fixed address or who live on the streets are not covered by these sampling frames. If such people are to be included in a survey as we have suggested they ideally should, alternative sampling frames have to be considered to augment that chosen for the general population. Although sampling from such groups requires no little effort and inevitably incurs additional expense, previous experience suggests this is an entirely feasible and worthwhile exercise where the subject of the research requires it.

---

[4] However, PAF does tend to yield comparatively high rates of deadwood (on average around 11 or 12%, although this varies by region) and this has to be allowed for when issuing a sample. Additionally there will some households in which no eligible person is resident; a small number of households will consist only of people below the minimum age for inclusion in the survey, and an estimated 30% will be households in which all residents are over 60 and who may be above the maximum age limit for inclusion. It is not possible to identify such households in advance, and the proportion of such addresses will of course rise as criteria of eligibility for inclusion in the survey become more stringent.

[5] There may be a further advantage to this method of sampling in a survey about a sensitive subject in that at least part of the randomising process is apparent to the householder when the interviewer makes the selection of individuals, thus helping to allay any fears about how respondents have been selected.

Institutions can be sampled using, for example, the List of Institutions which is maintained by the Vital Statistics branch of OPCS. The coverage of institutions provided by this frame has been evaluated by OPCS and has been found to be good in most respects, although its coverage of some establishments (for example places of detention) is not known. Alternatively, although requiring some additional administrative input, frames can be drawn up or obtained expressly for the purpose of the survey. Conducting the selection of individuals within institutions may, however, present complications in that prior agreement to approach individuals may have to be obtained from those in charge[6]. Response rates amongst respondents in institutions also tend to be generally lower than the average for the population as a whole.

There are various options for sampling homeless people, and space does not permit their discussion in full here. SCPR has recently carried out one of the few national surveys of such people, including both hostel users and rough sleepers, and achieved good response rates; 76% amongst those in temporary accommodation and 79% amongst rough sleepers (Lynn, 1992). Our experience is that although challenging, sampling of homeless people is certainly feasible.

Finally, it is worth noting that if special populations are to be included in a survey it is not necessary to sample proportionate to their representation in the population as a whole. Given that it is possible to obtain a reasonable estimate of the overall size of any given special population, for the purposes of a survey results from a non-proportionate sample can be extrapolated to give estimates for the special population as a whole.

Sample Size

As we have indicated in Section 1, a review of the various prevalence rates which large-scale studies have produced reveals a wide variation in estimates largely due to methodological and definitional differences between studies. In North American studies, prevalence rates found range from 6% to 62% for females and 3% to 31% for males (quoted in Finkelhor 1986). In British studies Baker and Duncan (1985) provide an estimate of 12% of females and 8% of males, as compared with Kelly et al. (1991) whose estimate ranges from 21% to 59% of females, and 7% to 27% of males dependent on definition. These variations make it difficult to estimate the sample size that would be required in a national survey of prevalence, and a large scale pilot using the

---

[6] During Phase Two of the study (depth interviews with known survivors of abuse), contacts with two inmates of a women's prison were made via the Probation Service. Both women expressed willingness to take part in a depth interview, but as an illustration of the difficulties of including such people in a survey, we found that we were unable to gain permission to conduct the interviews from the Board of Governors of the prison within the time available for the study.

recommended random sampling method will be required to provide firmer figures in this respect.

Nevertheless, it is possible to make some observations based on the prevalence rates found in other studies in Britain. The sample size that is required depends to a large extent on the type of analysis that will be undertaken. Generally speaking, the finer the level of analytical detail required, the larger the overall sample will need to be. Thus if there is to be meaningful analysis of sub-samples where base rates are likely to be low (for example, cases of abuse perpetrated by females, or certain types of abuse such as penetrative abuse), a larger overall sample will be needed in order to generate sufficient cases. If on the other hand analysis will focus broadly on overall prevalence and some supporting contextual detail, with little analysis of sub-samples, the overall sample size can be smaller.

For example, if we take Kelly's estimate of the prevalence of abuse by females (5% of adult perpetrators), and her lowest, most stringently defined estimate of prevalence (17% of females and males combined), we find that to generate approximately 100 cases of abuse by adult females the overall achieved sample would have to be 12,000 interviews. More conservatively still, if we wanted to look at intra-familial abuse of males based on Baker and Duncan's more conservative estimates of the prevalence of abuse (8% of males, of which 10% were intra-familial), we find an overall sample of 20,000 achieved interviews will be necessary to generate 80 cases. If, however, relatively little analysis of sub-groups were to be undertaken, using Kelly's maximal estimate of prevalence for men (27% before the age of 18), we find an overall sample of 8,000 achieved interviews will generate over 1,000 male cases comprised of various forms of abuse and unwanted sexual experiences, both contact and non-contact.

Questionnaire design

Designing a questionnaire which would be flexible and sensitive enough to capture the diversity of childhood sexual experiences, and specific enough to gather detailed information about their circumstances and context was one of the major challenges of the feasibility study. At each stage we had to consider not only how to present and and phrase such questions, but how to ensure that people would be willing to respond. Even if a relatively high overall response rate can be achieved in a survey of this kind, there is always the possibility that item response to individual questions on sexual experiences will be low, thus severely restricting the usefulness and reliability of the data. In fact, item response within the questionnaire was 100% for each of the four pre-pilots we carried out; despite the sensitivity and probing nature of some of the questions no respondent refused to answer a question. We attribute this to a combination of interviewer skill in building rapport with respondents and the careful design of the questionnaire.

Each of the four versions of the questionnaire used in successive pre-pilots drew heavily from the lessons learnt in the previous stage, with initial design informed by the depth interviews carried out in Phase Two of the study. Two issues dominated our thinking during the design of the questionnaire; on the one hand, the technical requirements of eliciting information about complex series of events in the distant past, and on the other the ethical considerations of asking people to recount personal and possibly traumatic memories. In particular, we felt issues of sensitivity to respondents' feelings and reactions to certain questions to be most important; we were concerned that the attempt to gather detailed, explicit, and technically sophisticated information about sexual experiences before 16 should not be at the expense of respondents' wellbeing; that the interview, although probing sensitive areas, should not leave respondents feeling threatened, uncomfortable or exploited; and that even the shyest respondent would feel sufficiently unembarrassed during the interview to be able to answer fully and frankly.

General issues of design and approach

The question of definition

As we have already discussed above in Sections 1 and 3, we attach great importance to the issue of definition of child sexual abuse. One of the problems of research in this field is the lack of comparability between the various definitions employed in different studies, making it hard to assess the reliability of prevalence estimates. Since the approach chosen by researchers necessarily conditions the information provided by respondents, one prevalence estimate may be measuring a very different phenomenon from another. Thus if the experiences asked about are pre-defined as "unwanted" or "abusive", with "adults" or "sexually mature" people or asked about only in the context of violent or traumatic situations, this will crucially affect the range of experience that is reported. Many writers have already discussed at some length and demonstrated practically the impact of theoretical and operational definitions on prevalence estimates; one effect which we were particularly concerned to avoid was that of respondents under-reporting certain sexual experiences because they did not share the research definition of a particular type of experience.[1]

Two issues therefore required careful consideration when operationalising the definition of sexual experiences used within the questionnaire. One was the need for comparability with other studies, and the other was the need to minimise potential restrictions on reporting by avoiding an overly prescriptive definitional framework. As we discuss below (see Module 6), our solution was to follow a two-stage approach to the collection of information on sexual experience. Firstly, to establish the incidence of sexual experiences, an operational definition was sought which would encompass definitions used in previous research, and which would allow the broadest possible range of experiences to be reported. Secondly, the quality of each experience reported was then explored in some depth, thus providing factual and perceptual detail which would allow experiences to be assessed within the various definitional frameworks used in other studies. Thus, for each experience reported we collected factual information on, for example, the age of the respondent and partner/perpetrator, the relationship of the partner/perpetrator to the respondent, the circumstances under which the sexual contact took place, and whether any form of coercion or incentive was used. Perceptual and attitudinal information was also collected: for example how respondents felt at the time, and what effects they perceived the experience to have had both in the short and long term. Using this method, it is possible to ensure that all the information necessary to make comparisons with other studies is readily available, be the definitional frameworks of other

---

[1] This is particularly the case where the research definition implies that the respondent was victimised by a particular experience. The tendency for people to resist defining themselves as victims is well documented (Finkelhor 1979; Berger et al 1988; Rausch and Knutson 1991; Knutson and Selner 1994), and is thought to apply particularly to males, for whom the victim role is incompatible with prevailing cultural ideologies of masculinity (Cherry 1991, Bolton et al. 1989, Finkelhor 1986). We found evidence to support this theory in the study; for example, the 12 year old boy who had had a sexual relationship with a 27 year old woman, and who defined this experience as sexually formative and very positive. Had the subject of the survey been presented as about "unwanted sexual experiences" or "child sexual abuse", it is unlikely he would have supplied any information about this experience, since he did not consider this experience either unwanted or abusive.

studies broad or narrow; for example, the data can be directly compared to those produced by other studies, where definitions are concerned with age differentials, relationships between actors, or the affective quality of the experience or indeed any combination of these.

Our overall approach to the issue of definition of sexual experiences is best described as 'minimum definition for maximum information': however, this is not simply a matter of giving respondents as little guidance as possible when soliciting information. Rather, it involves strenuous efforts to encourage respondents to resist self-censorship by emphasising the breadth of the range of experiences which are of interest to the study. It was found to be of vital importance that respondents were encouraged to think about 'sexual' experience in childhood in as broad a way as possible; that is, as involving *any* activity which they now believe to have had some sexual element *either* for themselves *or* for other people present (whether taking part or just watching), and as covering a wide range of possible activities, not just sexual intercourse.[2] We stressed that we were asking about a range of experiences, either wanted or unwanted, with same age, younger or older persons to ensure once again that as broad a definition of "sexual" experience as possible was employed by respondents. Using three show cards (see below), we provided specific examples of the kinds of sexual activities which might be included, taking care to word items on the cards so that both the passive and the active case was used, thus encouraging respondents to reflect on what they did to others as well as what was done to them[3]. It was also found that although superficially repetitive, this routine of screening questions and show cards needed to be followed each time a question on sexual experiences was asked, since respondents were apt to revert to employing narrow definitions in the absence of encouragement to do otherwise. Since we did not wish to collect information on lone sexual activity (for example, solitary masturbation, or solitary viewing of pornography) it was also important to stress that we only wanted to know about activities in which another person or persons were involved.

Seeking permission to probe for detail

Depth interviews with the survivors alerted us to the need for great care when probing for detail about sexual experiences in childhood; this evidence

---

[2] That members of the public frequently assume sexual activity to consist only of heterosexual intercourse itself has been shown in previous studies (Spencer et al. 1988); we found that even after giving a broader definition of sexual activity many times, as soon as the term "sexual contact" was used unqualified or undefined for respondents, some were apt to revert to thinking of this term as referring only to sexual intercourse. Therefore we found research definitions needed to be re-iterated each and every time the term was used.

[3] It was hoped that questions on sexual contact with others initiated by the respondent would provide some data regarding sexual victimisation perpetrated by same-age peers or older children.

informed both questionnaire design and interviewing technique during the feasibility study. To ensure the continuing co-operation of respondents, and to respect their sensibilities, interviewers were instructed to make it clear both in what they said, and in tone of voice, that they were asking *permission* to proceed. Questions were worded to indicate that the research team respected the fact that such information might be highly personal, but nevertheless regarded it as extremely valuable. The principle of confidentiality was re-iterated where there was any hesitation on the part of respondents, and the interviewer reminded them that they were at liberty to refuse to answer any question they felt uncomfortable about. For example, in pre-pilot 4 the detailed questions on sexual experience were prefaced with the following introduction, which was repeated before each new experience was asked about:

> "I'd like to ask you a little bit more about what happened when you had this sexual experience. I realise that this is a very personal and sensitive subject, but it is very important to know the circumstances these experiences occur in, and what effects they have on children and young people. Please just tell me as much as you feel able."

We found this 'softly-softly' approach paid dividends; in feedback several respondents commented that they appreciated the respect shown to their feelings when talking about possibly painful or embarrassing incidents, and felt more confident about the research and the interviewer's professional status as a result. Survivors of child sexual abuse were particularly likely to attach importance to this. In fact, far from encouraging people to refuse questions (as this type of approach might be thought to do), we feel that the excellent item response rate we achieved demonstrates that paying attention to respondents' feelings during the interview is a crucial aspect of encouraging full and frank disclosure in this sensitive area.[4]

The need for flexibility

Because the aim of the study was *not* simply to estimate the numbers of people who had particular types of experiences, but to explore in some depth

---

[4] There is, however, one caveat to this. One respondent answered negatively to all the screening questions, but was reported by the interviewer to appear somewhat discomfited. After the interview was over, the respondent told the interviewer that as a child she had been "sexually abused" *(sic)* by her step father, but that she did not wish to say any more about this. It is clearly important to recognise that though respondents may not actually refuse to answer a question, the response they give may not be accurate. We suspect that a proportion of respondents will, like this respondent, disclose CSA after the interview, and some steps to record such disclosures should be taken, even if detailed information cannot be collected (see Section 7). Furthermore, a proportion of respondents who have had abusive experiences may not disclose this at all. Once again, it must be acknowledged that prevalence rates obtained in a survey of this kind are likely to be underestimates of the true rate, because of the great difficulty which people may have in admitting to or talking about sexual victimisation.

the circumstances in which such experiences take place in order to further understanding of the nature and effects of different kinds of experiences, a very flexible instrument was needed in order to capture the full diversity of sexual activity before 16. Because the same questionnaire was to be used to collect information about both wanted, consensual experiences and unwanted, non-consensual ones great care had to be taken in the wording of questions so that they remained neutral, whilst at the same time did not appear to make light of what might have been very traumatic events for the respondent. As we have already commented in the context of flashing incidents in Section 3, an experience which is for one person trivial and unremarkable may for another person be highly disturbing and distressing. The data collection instrument must, therefore, be sufficiently sophisticated to take account of this in eliciting detail about the incident and its subsequent effect on the respondent; for example, the filters used are pivotal in terms of directing interviewers to one series of questions rather than another, and particular care must be taken in the design of these. (See below; Structure of the Incident Form.)

Furthermore, in the case of certain types of child sexual abuse, and particularly those which continue over long periods of time, there may be several changes in the circumstances in which the abuse occurs, each of which should be recorded. For example, the initial perpetrator may be joined by another person, other children may be drawn into the abuse, or the child's perception of the sexual contact may change from being a willing or perhaps indifferent partner to feeling increasingly coerced and unwilling. Ideally, the questionnaire should be able to record such changes in order that analysis can take place at a reasonably sophisticated level; indeed, such details are vital to understanding the significance of different experiences and to making sense of the data. Although it must be recognised that a quantitative study using a structured questionnaire is more limited in terms of the information that can be collected as compared with qualitative methods, we were able to develop a structured questionnaire that could, nevertheless, obtain detailed and complex data on this subject.

Questionnaire Design

Over the course of the four pre-pilots the design and content of each questionnaire changed considerably, as each pre-pilot yielded fresh insights into the methodological issues under investigation. We developed a modular design for the questionnaires used in the four pre-pilots so that each revised version could include certain standard core modules as well as introducing new modules of questions which were being tried for the first time. Therefore more questions were piloted in total than could probably be included in any one questionnaire for reasons of length. The various modules are described overleaf, with core modules indicated by an asterisk:

The Structure of the Questionnaire

Establishing context

*Module 1   **Current background/demographic details**

*Module 2   **Childhood circumstances**
(household composition, parents' occupation/social class, family finances etc.)

*Module 3   **Childhood family relationships**
(parents' relationship, respondent's relationships with key family members)

Module 4   **Other childhood relationships and friendships**

Asking about early sexual knowledge and experience

*Module 5   **First understanding and knowledge of growing up, sexual development and sex**
(early impressions of sex and extent of knowledge about sexual matters, attitudes within the home to sexual matters, level/content of formal sex education)

*Module 6
Separate
incident form
      Childhood sexual experiences
(circumstances and content of sexual experiences before 16, respondent's perceptions of quality of experience at time and subsequently, whether told anyone else)

*Module 7   **Attempts and narrow escapes before 16**
(unsuccessful/uncompleted attempts by others at sexual contact with respondent)

Collecting information about effects and outcomes

*Module 8   **Effects of sexual experiences before 16**
(immediate and long term sequelae of early sexual experiences)

Module 9
Self-completion
      Adult sexual experiences
(sexual contacts since 16, number/gender of partners, whether any coercive experiences, whether any sexual contact with minors)

Module 10
Self-completion
      Life events history
(checklist of life events before and after 16)

Module 11   **Adult physical and mental health**
(physical and mental health problems or disabilities, psychiatric morbidity, contact with therapeutic/counselling services)

Feedback

*Module 12   **Experiences of taking part in the interview**
Feelings about taking part in the study, reactions to questions, ease of recall, level of comfort with interviewer, general comments

---

* denotes core modules

As will be seen from this design, during the course of the four pre-pilots we covered a wide range of issues which are salient to the study of child sexual abuse, from the actual content and circumstances of sexual experiences before 16 to the long term sequelae in terms of adult functioning. We now discuss some of these modules in more detail.

Establishing Context

Questionnaire Modules 2, 3 and 4: Childhood and family circumstances

As we have discussed in Section 2, we found from our depth interviews that the overall context in which the study was presented, and the specific context in which individual questions were asked, played a very important role in encouraging people to talk frankly and fully about sensitive issues. Survivors of child sexual abuse demonstrated clearly that the sexual victimisation and exploitation of children can only be understood with reference to childhood experiences more generally; for example in the context of relationships within the family, patterns of childcare and upbringing and "access" to children, and attitudes to sexual matters and sex education within the home and at school. Only when these areas are explored can we begin to understand how children become vulnerable to abuse, and why once abused some children find themselves unable to tell anyone about what has happened, and may then become vulnerable to re-abuse.

We therefore devoted a large part of the questionnaire to establishing this context; building up a picture of the respondent's childhood circumstances and discussing various childhood relationships before moving on to specific questions related to sexual experience. Apart from providing important substantive information, there were also technical benefits to this approach. The careful reconstruction of childhood in terms of the chronology of significant events (for example, to pinpoint key life events such as the family moving house, the respondent changing schools, the birth of siblings or other changes in family structure) meant that later on in the interview, the important issue of the timing of particular sexual experiences was more easily established, because considerable attention had been paid to locating contextual "hooks" upon which such memories could be hung. Similarly, although discussing family relationships provided important information about the quality of childhood, there was an additional technical benefit to this approach. Because respondents had already spent some time discussing personal and sometimes sensitive memories with the interviewer, they had been given an opportunity to become 'acclimatised' to sensitive subject matter and used to talking in this way, before the even more sensitive subject of sexual experience was raised.

Asking about childhood sexual experience

Questionnaire Module 5: First understanding and knowledge of sexual development and sex

As we have said, item response to questions about actual childhood sexual experience was extremely high. One of the reasons for this was undoubtedly the gradual way in which respondents were led through questions of an increasingly sensitive and explicit nature, allowing them time to adjust to each level of sensitivity before moving on. This was achieved by prefacing questions on actual sexual experiences by a module of questions on first understanding and knowledge of growing up, sexual development and sex, in which the interviewer introduced sexual terms and concepts in the context of normative childhood experience. In this module, respondents were asked about a variety of issues: their parents' attitudes to sex, what they were told about physical and emotional aspects of sexual development, whether they discussed these things with adults or peers, how much they understood about sex before the age of 16, and what impressions they had formed, in advance of actual sexual activity, of what sex would be like. Interviewers very much took the lead in initiating discussion by introducing technical sexual terms and sexual language; this form of "permission giving" is known to be very important in obtaining information on sensitive or taboo subjects (Barton 1958; Spencer et al. 1988). Formal terms for anatomy and sexual acts were used by the interviewer at all times unless referring back specifically to language used by the respondent. Definitions of sexual terms were provided where necessary. The use of formal language has been found in other studies of sexual matters to be preferred by most respondents (Spencer et al. 1988); it also avoids vague or misleading euphemisms. We found that this was a relatively unthreatening way to begin talking about sexual experience; most respondents recalled being told (or more often *not* being told) the 'facts of life' by a parent or other family member, and the oblique, frequently baffling references to sex and sexuality offered in school sex education classes were remembered with some humour by many of those who were interviewed. Even respondents whose subsequent experiences of sex had been traumatic were usually able to talk in a relaxed way about their early knowledge or lack of knowledge of sexual matters generally, and this provided a smooth path into talking about particular experiences.

Questionnaire Module 6 and Incident Form : Childhood sexual experiences

Questions on sexual experiences themselves were administered using a separate 'Incident Form', one for each experience or series of experiences with the same person or persons. The trigger for an incident form to be completed was an affirmative response to any one of up to four screening questions, using show cards (see below) with code letters which described the broad range of types of experiences we wanted to explore. Screening questions used in this study included:

> "As well as what children and young people are *told* about growing up, sexual relationships and sex, it is also very important to know what they learn about these things from their own experiences. It is now realised that many people have experiences of a sexual kind before the age of 16, but little is known about what the range of experiences may be. These next few questions are about the early experiences which children and young people may have which can play an important part in growing up. **SHOW CARD J.** Looking at this card, thinking of the period before you were sixteen, can you remember having *any* experiences like this which, looking back, you would *now* consider to have been sexual? These experiences might have happened with a person of the same age as yourself, or a person of a different age, and might have been wanted, or unwanted by you."

and:

> "Apart from these experiences, you may have had different experiences before you were 16. These may have been things which you did not consider to be sexual at the time, but looking back you *now* realise were sexual in some way. Again, these experiences might have happened with a person of the same age as yourself, or a person of a different age, and might have been wanted, or unwanted by you.
>
> **SHOW CARD K** Looking at this card, can I ask, did you have *any* of the experiences listed here, or any similar experiences, before you were 16?"

and:

> "Looking at this card, did you have any of the experiences listed there, or any similar experiences before you were 16?" **SHOW CARD L**

and finally:

> "And may I just check, did you have any experiences before you were 16 which *you* do not consider to have been sexual, but which you think may have been sexual for someone else?" **SHOW CARD K**

The number of screening questions we asked increased over the course of the four pre-pilots; as other authors have noted (Finkelhor 1986; Kelly et al. 1991; Vizard 1989) the greater the number of screening questions, the higher the prevalence rate obtained will tend to be. This may be due to the fact that a greater number of screening questions allows the concept under investigation to be defined more fully and from different angles. Equally it may reflect the fact that some respondents require more encouragement to admit to, or recall, sexual experiences before 16 than others. The show cards were utilised at this early screening stage with actual examples of experiences people might have had, since the degree of specificity of screening questions is also thought to influence reporting (Finkelhor 1986, Vizard 1989), with greater specificity tending to produce higher prevalence rates.

Once an affirmative answer had been obtained at any of the screening questions, the interviewer then probed for detail on the experience, with each unit of experience being defined as **any one experience or series of experiences involving the same person or group of people.** Where respondents had had several such units of experience, the interviewer asked them to choose one to describe first, indicating that she would be giving them an opportunity to tell her about other experiences later in the interview. Thus respondents were not constrained as to the order in which they could talk about experiences with different partners or perpetrators, allowing those who needed to 'work up' to talking about a particular experience to do so. Analysis of the order in which respondents chose to tell interviewers about their various sexual experiences reveals no pattern; it appears that while some respondents will want to describe a particularly memorable unwanted experience first, others prefer to talk about wanted or non-traumatic experiences to start with, until they have developed sufficient rapport with the interviewer to feel able to talk about other less pleasant experiences.

Structure of the Incident Form

The Incident Form was structured around 'units' of experience, so that a new form was used to explore each experience or series of experiences involving the same person or group of persons. (See Figure 5.1 overleaf). Having established the number, age and gender of other people involved, the respondent was then shown a series of three further show cards on which a range of sexual activities were listed, each randomly assigned a code letter, and the respondent called out the relevant code letters to describe the sexual content of the experience or series of experiences. (An example of one of these cards is given on page 59). A very important filter question was then asked to establish whether or not the experience had been wanted or not, and on this basis respondents were asked a series of questions about the circum-

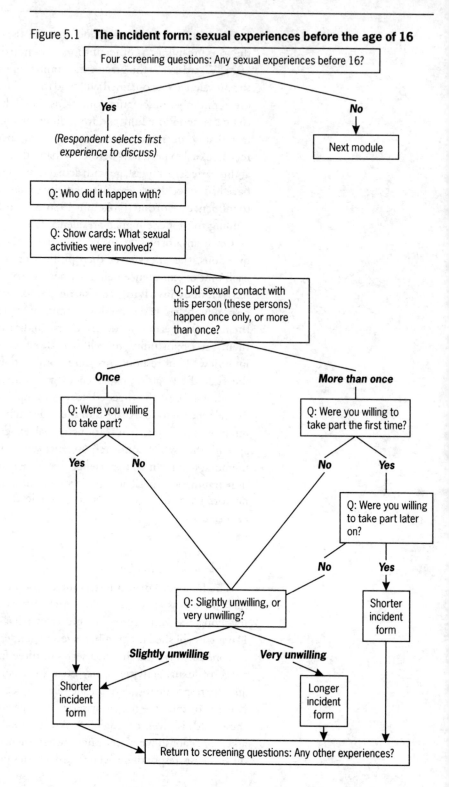

Figure 5.1   **The incident form: sexual experiences before the age of 16**

stances in which the incident or incidents had taken place. We avoided the problematic concept of 'consent', since a child may consent to something whilst at the same time not desiring or wanting the experience. This is an important aspect of child sexual abuse, since perpetrators have been reported to obtain the consent of a child to a particular act (often through some form of bribery or threat, or by 'grooming' for compliance (Finkelhor 1979, Berliner and Conte 1990; La Fontaine 1990; Singer et al. 1992), although the experience may remain unwanted by the child. Respondents were therefore asked whether they had been a willing participant in a particular incident or incidents, rather than whether or not they had consented.[5] The often subtle differences between degrees of willingness presented some challenges. In particular, perhaps reflecting prevailing cultural ideas about 'acceptable' sexual behaviour for girls and women, we found a tendency for women respondents to describe their sexual encounters with peers (usually defined as "boyfriends") as "unwilling". However, subsequent probing often revealed that the quality of the experience had in fact been largely mutual, usually consisting of various sexually exploratory acts over a period of time. Clearly, to categorize these kinds of experiences for the purpose of follow-up questions with other "unwilling" experiences such as rape, for example, makes little sense. Therefore in later pre-pilots degrees of willingness or unwillingness were probed in order to establish the appropriate series of follow-up questions. Experiences in which the respondent reported him or herself as consistently only *slightly* less willing than the other person involved triggered different sets of questions from those incidents which were reported as *very* unwillingly engaged in.

Answers to this filter determined the range of circumstantial questions which were subsequently asked, such as where and with whom the incident had occurred, whether or not anyone else knew of the event or was told about it, whether there were any outcomes (for example, were the police involved), and how the respondent had felt at the time. Somewhat more detail was collected about unwanted experiences than about consistently wanted experiences, in part due to pressure of time, since many more wanted experiences were reported than unwanted ones. Nevertheless, it should be noted that *all* experiences were probed to some level of detail, to account for incidents which might fall into research definitions of child sexual abuse even though the respondent regards the incident as willingly engaged in. Further-more changes in willingness over time were also probed and any experience which was at *any* time unwillingly engaged in was explored in substantial depth.

---

[5] See Finkelhor (1979) for further discussion of the inadequacy of the "consent standard of victimisation" in child sexual abuse research.

When all the relevant details pertaining to the experience had been collected, the respondent was then re-presented with the show cards and asked the series of screening questions again, and an affirmative answer to one or more sexual experiences with a different person triggered another Incident Form, and so on, up to a maximum of four Forms. Figure 5.1 shows the structure of the Incident Form diagrammatically.

The use of show cards

In order to explore the types of sexual experiences respondents had had before 16, we used a series of six show cards. These contained definitions of certain key terms, and covered a range of sexual activities, both contact and non-contact, from game-playing (such as 'doctors and nurses' and 'strip poker'), 'flashing', and viewing pornography through to various forms of sexual touching and intercourse. At the far end of the continuum were listed experiences such as rape, involvement in ritualised sexual activities, and sexual activities with animals. Each item on the card was randomly assigned a code letter which the interviewer instructed the respondent to call out if it applied to her or him. The show cards were divided into two different sets, and each set served a somewhat different purpose. The first set consisted of three cards which were used in conjunction with screening questions in order to establish whether or not respondents had had any sexual experiences before 16. The items which were listed on these three cards were loosely worded in such a way as to cover a range of similar activities; they were intended to stimulate memory and indicate the range of activities to be considered rather than provide very specific and detailed information on sexual experiences. The second set of cards were shown to the respondent after the incidence of sexual experiences had been established. These three cards covered a wider and more detailed range of sexual acts, and were used to determine the exact content of respondents' sexual experiences before 16.

An example of one screening card used with the screening questions is shown opposite:

Example (1) Screening Card K

P1217/P4

CARD K   WOMEN

Genitals: *a person's private parts or sex organs (a man's penis, a woman's vagina)*

Masturbation: *touching or rubbing genitals in order to achieve sexual arousal and orgasm (climax)*

K8	Someone exposed their genitals to you or 'flashed' at you
K10	You were made to watch sexual activities between other people
K2	Someone showed you pornographic (blue/adult/X-rated) pictures, photographs or videos
K1	Someone other than a "boyfriend" or girlfriend" asked you to do something sexual to them, or asked to do something sexual to you
K3	Someone other than a "boyfriend" or "girlfriend" touched or fondled you in a sexual way
K7	Someone other than a "boyfriend" or "girlfriend" kissed you in a sexual way
K4	Someone pressed or rubbed their genitals against you
K6	Someone masturbated you
K9	Someone masturbated in front of you
K12	Someone put their mouth on your genitals or anus (back passage)
K13	Someone put their finger or an object in your vagina or anus
K5	Someone put his penis inside your vagina or anus
K11	Someone raped you or attempted to rape you

Reactions to the show cards

Feedback indicated that although initially some respondents were somewhat taken aback or embarrassed by the explicit nature of the cards, most recognised the legitimacy of asking for detail of this kind in the context of the survey, and were not offended by being asked to read them. We asked all respondents whether they had found any part of the interview offensive, and out of 127 interviews only two respondents had strong adverse reactions to the cards; both these people commented that they were not so much offended by the items on the cards as the idea that people under sixteen could be involved in such activities. By contrast, several respondents specifically praised the cards; the code lettering system meant that neither respondent nor interviewer was ever required to name the specific activities, and most respondents said they felt this had made it much easier for them to answer honestly.[6] We chose to be as explicit as possible in order to explore the outer limits of the information which can be collected in a survey; however, it may not be necessary to go to the level of detail that we did, since low base rates for some activities would probably result in combining categories for analysis. Nevertheless, we feel we have demonstrated that given the right approach, a very high level of specificity can be achieved if desired.

Questionnaire Module 7: "Uncompleted" sexual contact

Kelly et al. (1991) have stated the importance of including a question which taps incidents involving attempted and uncompleted sexual contact. Our findings support this, and suggest that if a respondent had managed to avoid sexual unwanted contact, for example by running away, or because an attempt at contact was interrupted, these incidents initially may not be reported. We were alerted to this possibility early on in the pre-pilots, when a respondent answered negatively to all the questions on sexual experiences, but then inquired of the interviewer whether or not an attempted rape "counted" as a sexual experience. Our subsequent inclusion of **Module 7**, a module of questions on attempted or uncompleted sexual experiences yielded a further nine descriptions of unwanted experiences of a serious nature, including a molestation on a bus, several apparent attempted abductions including one of a boy of 11 by two men, a violent attempted rape and various incidents of indecent exposure and fondling.

Collecting information on effects and outcomes

Modules 8 to 11 contained questions designed to shed light on the question of the short and long-term effects of certain types of sexual experiences in childhood. There are various ways in which these subjects can be approached, including a number of standard measures used to assess physical and mental health such as those often used in surveys in the general

---

[6] Survivors told us in depth interviews (where cards were not, of course, used) that one of the most difficult things for them was to actually name what had been done to them sexually. Some of them found this so distressing as to be physically impossible, and thus the coded cards system overcomes this first and most crucial hurdle in the interview process. As part of testing the structured questionnaires some survivors were re-interviewed later in the study, and they particularly endorsed the used of show cards for this purpose.

population (for example the General Health Questionnaire; Goldberg 1972), the health problems and disabilities question used in the General Household Survey conducted by OPCS, and the Beck Depression Inventory (Beck et al. 1961). Additionally, there are measures often used in clinical work with survivors of child sexual abuse such as the Trauma Symptom Checklist (Briere and Runtz 1987), the Hopkins Symptom Checklist (Derogatis et al. 1974), the Minnesota Multiphasic Personality Inventory (MMPI) (Friedrich 1988) and the Texas Social Behaviour Inventory (TSBI), (Helmreich and Stapp, 1974).

After consideration more specialised clinical measures were felt to be unsuitable because of the heterogeneous nature of the sample in terms of the experience of victimisation, and because these measures are often unsuited to administration in a large scale survey where data collection is by field interviewers rather than clinicians. We therefore chose to use a mixture of open-ended questions and fixed choice questions especially developed for the study, in combination with standard measures in order to maintain comparability with other general population studies wherever possible.

Questionnaire Module 8: Respondents' perceptions of short and long-term effects

Module 8 included a short series of simply-worded open-ended questions which asked respondents to assess the effects of particular early sexual experiences on them both at the time and in the longer term. These questions were open-ended partly because experience with survivors suggested that after a long series of structured questions which can inevitably capture only the basic facts of the particular experience, some respondents clearly felt the need of the opportunity to talk in their own words about their feelings. The potential diversity of answers given here also made pre-coding undesirable at this stage.

Questionnaire Module 9: Adult sexual history

Module 9 was a short self-completion supplement concerning adult sexual experiences. This collected brief information on sexual history after the age of 16, including number and gender of partners, experience of sexual victimisations, and of paying—or being paid for—sex. Information about respondents' sexual contacts in adulthood with minors was also collected here, with a small number of respondents (four in total) saying they had had such contact. A national survey of this kind would appear to present an ideal opportunity to obtain information on adult-child sexual contact which we feel should not be missed, given the current debate about the intergenerational transmission of abuse. (e.g. Herzberger 1993). However, as we received only a few positive answers, and did not attempt to collect any detailed information on the circumstances in which such contact had taken place, we would recommend that a larger-scale pilot explore this further, in particular considering issues connected with validity of the data.

Questionnaire Module 10: Life events history

Clinical studies of the longer term effects of child sexual abuse have often inferred causal links between abuse and problems in adult life, for example with physical and mental health, without measuring other stressors which may impact on adult functioning. Studies which have investigated the physical, psychological and social outcomes of abuse have undertaken all kinds of sophisticated modelling to assess the relative contribution of different aspects of abuse, for example the duration of the abuse, the relationship to the abuser, and whether the abuse was disclosed (Briere and Runtz 1988; Beitchman et al. 1992), but the contribution of other life events to the outcomes being measured is rarely considered. However, the apparent causal link between having been sexually victimised in childhood and say, attempting suicide, may seem much less clear if one knows that the person has also suffered many other stressful life events in addition to child sexual abuse such as bereavement, loss of a job, problems with money and so forth. Some life events such as repeated relationship breakdowns may be thought to be related to the experience of abuse itself (Conte and Schuerman 1987); however others, such as bereavement, may be regarded as independent variables.

For this reason we think it important to include, as we did in **module 10**, a short life events history in which other potential stressors in the life of respondents apart from child sexual abuse can be assessed. This was administered as a self-completion supplement, with questions in the check list based on the Holmes and Rahe (1967) Social Readjustment Rating Scale scale, and divided into the two time frames; before 16 years and since the age of 16.

Questionnaire Module 11: Adult physical and mental health

Finally, we included a module of questions (**module 11**) to provide data which speak to the association between childhood sexual experiences and adult physical health problems and psychiatric morbidity. A standard checklist of physical and mental health problems and disabilities was used to provide comparability with general population data, followed by a series of questions developed over the course of the four pre-pilots aimed at assessing mental health problems. Again, some of these questions were very sensitive in nature (we included questions on, for example, history of eating disorders, suicidal fantasies and suicide attempts, and contact with psychiatric or counselling services); but item response was 100%.

Interview Length

Because of the sensitive nature of the subject matter, for both ethical and technical reasons, we feel that an average interview length of no less than one hour would be required. Although interviews should not be longer than absolutely necessary for reasons of cost, as well as respondent and interviewer fatigue, we believe attempts to condense this type of interview ultimately will be counter-productive. We feel that the high item response we achieved, and the apparently frank way in which respondents answered very personal questions was made possible by allowing sufficient time for interviewer and respondent to establish a good rapport, and by approaching the more sensitive questions slowly and gradually. Analysis of the interview lengths across the four pre-pilots shows a wide range, with survivors tending to take longer to interview. Data on actual interview lengths in the four pre-pilots will be found in the Technical Appendix to this report; average length ranged from 79 minutes in pre-pilot 2[7] to 47 minutes in the final pre-pilot, where a smaller range of questions were included in the questionnaire. The average interview length for the pre-pilots as a whole was 65 minutes. The number of Incident Forms allowed per respondent for recording details of childhood sexual experiences will obviously affect interview lengths. We allowed a maximum of four Forms per respondent, although in practice only one interview required the completion of all four, and the average per respondent for the last two pre-pilots (in which screening questions were more stringent than previously) was less than one Form (0.7 in pre-pilot 3, 0.8 in pre-pilot 4). We would not, however, recommend an allowance of less than three Forms, as this would severely reduce the number of incidents reported. Additionally, the biasing effect of limiting respondents to less than three Forms is unknown, given that the pattern in which experiences are disclosed or recalled is not clear. Again, a full-scale pilot could investigate this further.

---

[7] This figure includes interviews with 4 known survivors who had already participated in qualitative interviews who kindly took part in order to permit full testing of the semi-structured questionnaire.

Mode of administration

Previous researchers in the field have utilised a variety of different modes of administration in surveys of the prevalence of child sexual abuse. In the United States, where research into child sexual abuse has been taking place for some years, telephone interviewing methods, postal surveys, supervised self-completion and face-to-face interviewing have been used in the past (Finkelhor 1979; Finkelhor et al. 1990; Russell 1984; Lewis 1985; Kercher and McShane 1984) and in this country both face-to-face interviews and self-completion methods (both postal and supervised) have been used recently to ask questions on sexual victimisation. (Baker and Duncan 1985; Nash and West 1985; Kelly et al. 1991)

The method selected is very much conditioned by the level of detail required. We chose a predominantly face-to-face mode of administration for the questionnaire, since experience has demonstrated that this is the method most suited to the collection of quantitative data which is both complex and sensitive. Short self-completion supplements were incorporated where the type of data required indicated this, and both methods were evaluated on an ongoing basis throughout the feasibility study.

Self-completion methods

If only a few questions are to be asked about childhood sexual experiences, perhaps restricted to specific and tightly defined types of experience, then self-completion, either in a postal survey or supervised by an interviewer, may be appropriate. Additionally, Kelly has argued recently that self-completion methods may have advantages over face-to-face interviewing in that more privacy is afforded to the respondent. (Kelly et al. 1991a) We feel, however, that the resultant loss of sophistication of the questionnaire, the increase in response error, and the decrease in item response are a high price to pay for this. Self-completion schedules have to be kept very simple and largely unfiltered, relatively short, and are prone to high levels of item non-response (Brook 1977). A recent study comparing the use of postal and face-to-face methods in a survey of childhood sexual experiences amongst adult women illustrates this well (Martin et al. 1993). Although the authors are of the opinion that "the anonymity of a written response may be a positive influence on disclosure" (p389), they go on to describe how face-to-face interviews were necessary to clarify certain answers from the written questionnaire, and that this resulted in some level of recoding of types of sexual experiences. We ourselves found some tentative evidence to suggest that prevalence rates for child sexual abuse collected by self-completion methods are likely to be lower than those yielded by face-to-face interviewing; of 29 respondents who completed a life events checklist which included the statement "You were sexually abused as a child", only one answered affirmatively to this. In the main interview, however, 10 of these 29 respondents reported sexual experiences in childhood which they described as unwanted and which would fall into many research definitions of abuse.

Additionally, self-completion methods are biased against respondents with literacy problems, and since it has been suggested that poor educational performance may result from the experience of child sexual abuse (CIBA Foundation 1984), it would seem dangerous to chose a main method of administration which is biased in this way. For these reasons, we do not advocate this as a main method of data collection. Unsupervised self-completion methods are certainly not recommended, since they too easily invite poor response, and may create problems of confidentiality.

Supervised self-completion schedules may, however, be useful as an efficient way of collecting supplementary data in certain parts of the interview, which are perhaps peripheral to the main subject of the survey, and about which much detailed data collection cannot be justified. This method was used in the National Survey of Sexual Attitudes and Lifestyles to ask more detailed questions about sexual history and current behaviour (Johnson et al. 1993) and in the British Crime Survey to ask about drug use (Hales 1993), among other examples. In the feasibility study, we used this method to ask about life events history and to gather brief data about adult sexual experiences.

Telephone interviewing

Although telephone interviewing does allow for a more sophisticated questionnaire and the collection of more detail on the survey variables than self-completion methods and does not require the respondent to be literate, again, we feel the level of detail that can be collected in a face-to-face interview is not approached. Although there may be an argument for the greater anonymity afforded to respondents in a telephone interview, which may increase the likelihood of frank responses to sensitive questions, we feel that any gains made here will be offset by the lack of rapport which the interviewer can build with the respondent, and the ease with which the respondent can terminate the interview should he or she become uncomfortable with the questions. Additionally, the interviewer cannot ensure that the necessary conditions of privacy are maintained during the interview, which may affect item response, particularly on open-ended questions. In the USA, telephone interviews have tended to include only a minority of relatively simple questions on actual sexual experiences, bedded in questions on less sensitive subjects such as public attitudes to child sexual abuse; we feel that the problems cited above, combined with the technical problems of telephone interviewing (for example poor coverage within the UK population for certain groups, association for women respondents with obscene calls, and the difficulty of demonstrating confidentiality to respondents) make telephone interviewing techniques unsuitable for this type of survey.

Face-to-face interviewing

The level of detail and the high quality of the data we were able to collect convinced us that face-to-face interviewing remains the best mode of administration for a survey of this kind, provided interviewers are properly trained and aware of their own potential for influencing respondents. Feedback from respondents reassured us that interviewers had been able to establish sufficient rapport to enable full and frank responses; only a small proportion of respondents (5%) indicated that they had not been as frank as they might have been with the interviewer, and comments both to interviewers and to researchers[1] revealed that respondents had felt relaxed and comfortable with interviewers, often to their own surprise.

There are, however, certain important conditions which must be satisfied for face-to-face interviewing to succeed. Interviewer training and interviewer effects have been mentioned already, and are discussed in more detail in Section 8; another important fieldwork issue is the desirability of ensuring privacy for respondents. Although private interviewing conditions are always desirable in high quality survey research, they are, we feel, especially so in a survey of this nature. The ethical dilemmas inherent in interviewing young people if parents are in the vicinity have already been referred to; additionally, respondents cannot be expected to answer questions on their personal sexual history in the presence of partners or children or indeed any third party. Interviewers working on the four pre-pilots made strenuous efforts to obtain a private space in which to conduct the interview; in a few cases they did not succeed, and anecdotal evidence suggests that the potential for embarrassment and for respondents to take exception to the questions is much greater in these situations. We also have grave doubts as to the reliability of data collected in the presence of a third party. This means that fieldwork procedures have to be flexible enough to allow interviewers either to postpone appointments until the respondent knows they will be able to find a private space in the home, which may involve rather longer than usual fieldwork periods, or if this is not possible, to allow alternative venues for

---

[1] All respondents were given an (anonymised) 'comment slip' and pre-paid envelope at the end of the interview, and invited to send any further comments they had about the interview or the survey direct to the research team.

interviewing to take place. Some surveys which require unusual data to be collected—for example, the Allied Dunbar National Fitness Survey (Health Education Authority and the Sports Council 1992) in which a physical fitness test was undertaken by respondents—have utilised alternative venues for interviews and other procedures, and some similar arrangements would be desirable in a survey of this kind. We suggest that respondents who cannot be private in their own home be offered the possibility of an interview elsewhere in the local area (for example, in the function room of a local hotel); some incentive payment to cover expenses might be required in addition, and transport might need to be provided. However, even were alternative venues readily available, we recognize that in the context of a major national survey a certain proportion of respondents may well be unwilling to be interviewed away from home. Furthermore, evidence from the feasibility study shows that some people are unwilling to be interviewed in private, either because they feel more comfortable with a family member or friend present, or because they feel it will cause offence to, or friction with, their spouse or partner. In these situations even the most tactful and persuasive interviewers may find it difficult to obtain the necesaary conditions of privacy. Although in the feasibility study we did not exclude respondents who were unwilling to be interviewed in private, it might well be that in a national survey interviewers would be advised to discontinue an interview under these circumstances.

Accuracy, Reliability and Validity

Memory and recall: facts

The problem with any retrospective survey which asks about distant events is that the accuracy of information given may be undermined by failure or distortions in recall. In the feedback module, nearly half of the respondents (48%) said they had some difficulty in remembering certain aspects of their childhood, with the pre-school period being cited most frequently. Thus data on the period between birth and four or five years old may be subject to more distortion than other data about later events, and this must be borne in mind during analysis. However, as we have said, we found that with care, for most people contextual 'hooks', usually key life events (for example, starting school, moving house, or the birth of a brother or sister) could be established which helped respondents to assign ages to other key events that the survey was concerned with, such as the age at which various sexual experiences occurred. Although it was not always possible to pin key facts to precise ages, particularly when the pre-school period was involved, it was usually possible for interviewers to obtain an estimate which would enable the location of events within reasonably tight age bands.

Memory and recall: perceptions

Perceptual recall is also subject to distortion in a retrospective survey, and in this case is particularly likely to be affected by intervening adult rationalisations. Where child perceptions rather than adult ones are required, extra effort must be made to assist respondents to provide the right sort of information. For example, we found in talking to survivors that a considerable amount of effort had to be made, by interviewer and respondent alike, to overcome the tendency for adult post-hoc rationalisations to obscure the memory of child perceptions. This was particularly the case when survivors had been in counselling or therapy for a long time, and were used to looking back on their experiences with an informed and politicised perspective. Although we do not believe this to be an insurmountable problem, again it indicates that interviews must be of sufficient length to permit the respondent to work back through adult perceptions to child perceptions, and question wording and interviewers must be sensitive to the need to constantly remind respondents to think of how they felt at the time of the event in question, if that is the information required.

One difficulty which must be acknowledged with both factual and perceptual recall on the subject of childhood is the tendency for painful, traumatic or deeply confusing events in childhood to be suppressed or "blocked", as a form of psychological coping mechanism. This blocking mechanism has been well described in the literature on survivors of child sexual abuse, (Bass and Davies 1990, Bolton et al. 1989, Women's Research Centre, Vancouver 1989, Blume 1985).[1] The clinical literature indicates that some people who have been the victims of child sexual abuse may have no memory at all of the abuse, and that some victims may have only partial memory. Additionally, we found that across the four pre-pilots for the feasibility study, somewhat under 10% of respondents reported problems of recall with specific reference to sexual experiences, some claiming that memories an unpleasant nature had been deliberately suppressed. For example, one respondent explained that she had had difficulty recalling the details of an experience of violent attempted rape; as she put it, "I suppose because I wanted to block it out."

As indicated earlier, this has the potential to affect the a survey interview in one of two ways. Firstly, if a proportion of memories of child sexual abuse are blocked like this, prevalence rates gained by a survey may be affected both by artificially low numbers of respondents admitting to certain experiences, and an artificially low number of reported experiences per respondent. The order by which prevalence rates may be reduced by this phenomenon cannot be estimated. Secondly, the survey interview itself may act as an "unblocking" or triggering mechanism in some cases. Evidence that this is the case was found in depth interviews with survivors, many of whom uncovered new memories as they talked to the interviewer, and it was also found in callback interviews with survey respondents, two of whom had recalled childhood sexual experiences of some significance subsequent to the interview[2]. The fact that memories of sexual experiences may be retrieved *after* the survey interview suggests that it might be very important from the point of view of obtaining more accurate prevalence estimates to provide for a second round of data collection after the initial interview. This could involve a follow-up of the sample as a whole or some proportion of the sample, and could be achieved by a second, much briefer interview a few days after the first interview, by postal self-completion questionnaire, or by telephone callback.

Additionally, the recovery of traumatic memories in this way of course raises ethical issues; interviewers must be trained to cope with the very vivid 'flashbacks' which have been reported to occur in some survivors, and which

[1] Indeed we were provided with a graphic example of this by one of our survivors, who had been very brutally raped as a twelve year old, and had suppressed the memory of the event—as she described it—almost as it happened. This woman had only recovered this memory for the first time whilst in hypnotherapy for emotional difficulties in her fifties.

[2] One woman recalled, during subsequent discussions about the survey with family, that she had been encouraged to fondle and hold an uncle's penis on several occasions when she was about four years old; another (male) respondent remembered that an older man had fondled his genitals on one occasion.

can be most distressing for survivor and interviewer alike. Consideration must be given to the most appropriate way to support respondents who are subject to this or who may be in any other way traumatised by the interview process, through adequate interviewer training and preparation, and through the provision of contact telephone numbers where help and counselling can be obtained. We discuss this further in Sections 8 and 9. The need to avoid the survey interview becoming a form of further abuse of survivors cannot be too strongly emphasised.

Reliability and Validity

Apart from genuine failures and distortions of memory, the likelihood that traumatic, painful, embarrassing or socially unacceptable events may be systematically under-reported in some conscious way, whilst other experiences may be over-reported cannot be overlooked. Evidence from the National Survey of Sexual Attitudes and Lifestyles (Johnson et al. 1992) found that women tended to under-report sexual contacts, whilst men tended to exaggerate, reflecting prevailing contemporary social and cultural beliefs about masculine and feminine sexual roles. A different effect has been observed when the issue is specifically the incidence of sexual victimisation, with men being less likely than women to report victimisations because the sexual victim role is not readily compatible with prevailing concepts of masculinity, and particularly heterosexual masculinity (Finkelhor 1979, Bolton et al. 1989), but with women also tending to under-report these types of experiences.

Although we acknowledge that some level of *under-reporting* of child sexual abuse is likely to be found for both sexes, we have endeavoured to overcome this by adopting a value-neutral approach which does not pre-define experiences as "victimising", and which makes it possible for respondents of both sexes to report experiences with any label they choose attached to that experience.[3] The use of multiple screening questions also promotes opportunity to disclose embarrassing or painful memories, as would the use of follow-up techniques. Well-trained interviewers, and offering respondents the possibility of talking to either a female or a male interviewer also help to encourage openness (see below Section 8). Furthermore, we incoporated a question on how frank the respondent had felt able to be, and whether there was anything of relevance which had not been disclosed to the interviewer. Feedback from respondents was encouraging in this respect, with only 6 respondents across the four pre-pilots (out of a total of 127 people inter-

---

[3] Thus one man described sexual contacts between himself at the age of twelve with a woman of twenty-seven and attached very positive labels to this experience, and several men described sexual advances made towards them by adults which they had not by any means welcomed, but which they did not regard as victimising in any way.

viewed) saying they had not been completely frank. Also reassuring was the fact that when probed for clarification, all 6 said there had only been "a few" things they had held back, rather than "a lot". The evidence from the study therefore suggests that with care, it is possible to minimise under-reporting to a significant extent. However, actual levels of under-reporting cannot be quantified, of course.

We do not think that deliberate *over-reporting* is a significant problem; we can see no advantage to a respondent to over-report childhood sexual contacts (particularly non-consensual or unwanted ones) in a confidential survey of this kind. Although it is known that males tend to over-estimate their number of sexual contacts, the evidence for this has come from studies of adult sexual behaviour where consent on the part of the respondent is assumed to exist. Therefore we suspect this 'exaggeration effect' is likely to apply only to 'wanted' sexual encounters; 'unwanted' sexual encounters are more likely to be regarded as stigmatising by males, and as discussed earlier, the problem here lies with under, not over reporting.

As regards non-deliberate over-reporting, recently there has been some concern about a phenomenon dubbed "false memory syndrome". (See for example Simon Hoggart, writing in The Observer Magazine 27th March 1994.) This is described as a situation in which an adult person 'remembers' fictious incidents of child sexual abuse, often describing memories which have been uncovered under the guidance of a therapist of uncertain pedigree. The 'victim' may have very vivid memories and be genuinely convinced of the truth of the allegations he or she has made. It is not known whether this phenomenon is widespread (most of the recently publicised cases have occurred in the USA where therapy and analysis are rather more common than they are in Britain). However, practitioners working with survivors of abuse have stressed that speculation about the significance of so-called false memory syndrome must be seen in the context of substantial and long-standing research evidence which shows that it is not uncommon for adults to recover memories of abuse many years after the actual events (Herman and Schatcow 1986), and that furthermore there appears to be far more weighty evidence in favour of under-reporting of abuse and suppression of memories than of over-reporting and fabrication (Summit 1983). They point out that it is in the nature of child sexual abuse that allegations are frequently impossible to substantiate to the standards required in law, since witnesses are rare and forensic evidence frequently unobtainable. Furthermore, as in cases of false accusation, many proven pepetrators will deny vehemently their involvement in child sexual abuse and will seek strenuously for alternative explanations of an allegation, even when the balance of evidence is clearly against them (Mathews, Matthews and Speltz 1989; Gracewell Institute, personal com-munication). Clearly reliable research into false memory syndrome is required. In the mean time we would suggest that in a full scale prevalence survey questions about the manner and context in which adult memories of child sexual abuse were recovered could be incorporated into the questionnaire, to provide information on this important aspect of disclosure. This said, however, since our depth interviews clearly showed that one of the greatest fears of any survivor of child sexual abuse is of not being believed, the methodological 'need' for such questions would have to be weighed against the ethical implications of risking causing further distress and trauma to genuine survivors.

Finally, construct validity is assumed to be high. We paid careful attention to the elaboration of the concept of "sexual experience", with all the experiences described by respondents considered by them to be sexual to some degree. We are therefore confident that we have good measures of childhood sexual experience.

Interviewer training and deployment

In the light of arguments in favour of the use of face-to-face interviewing modes (see Section 6), and evidence from other studies suggesting the advantages of personal interviews being conducted by well trained and sympathetic interviewers (Russell 1984; Wyatt 1985; and Nash and West 1985), the feasibility study set out to evaluate a number of aspects of the preparation, training, assessment and deployment of survey interviewers.

Preparation and training

We placed considerable emphasis on the preparation and training of the interviewers who took part in each of the four pre-pilot studies described in this report. Most important was the development of a neutral but sympathetic approach, without a hint of embarrassment or criticism. Although these qualities are a requirement for any survey, they would appear to be of particular significance for a study of child sexual abuse, where the events reported may well lie outside interviewers' own experiences, and consequently be the cause of distress or disapproval. Indeed, during the course of the depth interviews with adult survivors of sexual abuse it was made very clear to us that the attitude and manner of interviewers would be crucial to the success or failure of the survey, determining whether or not people would agree to take part in the study as a whole, or to answer particular questions. This confirmed evidence from previous studies which suggests that well trained interviewers who can establish a good rapport with respondents are more likely to achieve higher figures both for participation and for the reporting of childhood sexual experiences (Russell 1984).

Eight of the most experienced female SCPR interviewers were chosen to take part in the feasibility study. All had many years' experience of working in social survey research on both non-sensitive and sensitive subjects, interviewing both special populations as well as working on surveys of the general population. Additionally, all of the interviewers had worked on the Survey of Sexual Attitudes and Lifestyles (Johnson et al. 1994); some had encountered adult survivors of abuse during the course of that study. However, in view of the extreme sensitivity of the subject matter of this study, in addition to this experience we felt that special preparation and training would be advisable.

In order to devise an appropriate training and briefing programme, we sought advice from the staff of SCOSAC (Standing Committee on the Sexual Abuse of Children), who agreed to act as consultants in this regard. Together with SCOSAC, SCPR devised and mounted an initial familiarisation and training day, followed by a full day's briefing for each of the four pre-pilot studies.

All of the interviewers involved in the feasibility study attended the initial training and preparation session, which comprised the following modules:

- an introduction to the purpose of the feasibility study
- an introduction to the subject of child sexual abuse (theories, facts and figures)
- the nature of child sexual abuse (the range and types of experience)
- survivors' accounts[1]
- aspects of the disclosure process
- short and long term effects
- support and feedback for the interviewers themselves[2]

The aim of these modules was to make sure that interviewers understood the diversity of experiences and behaviours which may be considered as constituting child sexual abuse, whilst at the same time exploring their own preconceptions, beliefs and experiences.[3] Interviewers claimed to have found these sessions very valuable, especially the videos of survivors' own accounts, as they extended their knowledge and understanding of abuse, prepared them for the kind of information they might elicit, and gave them insight into survivors' feelings and sensibilities.

In each of the four pre-pilots, a further day of preparation consisted of a thorough briefing on the sample design and method, the approach(es) to be used for presenting the study to potential respondents, and a complete dummy run through all the question modules to be evaluated. Because of their wide-ranging experience, the interviewers were able to contribute extensively at these briefing sessions, and with their collaboration we were able to modify the questionnaire and make revisions to the text of explanatory letters and doorstep introductions.

---

[1] Training videos were shown, in which survivors recounted the circumstances and effects of their experiences of child sexual abuse.

[2] Phone numbers for members of the SCPR research team were supplied to the interviewers in case they needed support or debriefing after particularly difficult or distressing interviews. Whilst this was adequate for the pre-pilot studies because of the small number of interviews involved, a more comprehensive support system would be required for a large scale national survey. SCOSAC have agreed to explore the possibility of setting up of a network of helplines should these prove necessary.

[3] In any large field force it is likely that at least some of the interviewers will have had childhood experiences which could be considered sexually abusive. It is particularly important, therefore, that interviewers should have an opportunity to examine their feelings about these experiences before embarking on a study of the issue.

Assessment

Wherever possible, pre-pilot interviews were audio-taped with the permission of respondents, and in each case tapes were compared with completed questionnaires in order to assess the accuracy of interviewer coding, as well as the flow and ease of the interview. These recordings provided insight into technical aspects of the interview process, but more importantly they helped to evaluate the extent to which interviewer and respondent appeared to be at ease during the interview itself. In addition to listening to the tapes, a full day's debriefing was carried out after each of the four pre-pilot stages, and interviewers' observations about respondents' reactions were discussed at length.

Evidence from both the tapes and the debriefings reveals that a good level of rapport can be achieved even on a subject as sensitive as child sexual abuse, and that interviewer performance and skills improve over time as interviewers become more comfortable and familiar with both the subject matter and the questionnaire.[4] Establishing such rapport does indeed appear to depend on a thorough programme of preparation and training, and on the opportunity to develop and refine interviewing skills in the field.

Deployment

The issue of deployment covers the choice and selection of interviewers, both in terms of their expertise and experience, and in the light of the possible effects of particular interviewer characteristics on the disclosure of sensitive material.

In the first place, it is our contention that ideally only known and experienced interviewers should be used for a study of this kind. This argument is based on the nature and complexity of the subject matter which requires sensitive and professional handling. Using known and trusted interviewers also takes account of the need to ensure that people with a personal agenda in relation to child sexual abuse, for example perpetrators or victims, cannot gain access to the field force for this particular study. Of course, a large interviewing resource such as that available to SCPR may already include both adult survivors and perpetrators of abuse, but the fact that they are known to the organisation and have worked on numerous other studies does at least mean that they will not have deliberately targeted a study of abuse. In a main survey, additional screening (for example, checking for criminal records) could also be carried out to identify perpetrators amongst the field force. However, as many perpetrators remain undetected (Evertsz 1992), this procedure could not be regarded as a definitive check.

---

[4] This can also be inferred from the increase in response between pre-pilots 3 and 4.

As discussed above, throughout the feasibility study only the most senior and experienced of SCPR interviewers were invited to take part. On the basis of this experience, we would advocate that long standing members of the field force be used for a national survey, but recognise that an exercise on the scale of the recent study of sexual attitudes and lifestyles would make heavy demands on existing interviewers. If it proved necessary to recruit new members of the field force, we would advise a phased and gradual recruitment programme, to allow for the screening, induction, and familiarisation of new interviewers.

On the question of the possible influence of interviewer characteristics on the disclosure of experiences of child sexual abuse, it was necessary in the feasibility study to consider the advantages and disadvantages of some kind of matching between interviewer and respondent, particularly in relation to gender. Evidence from the development work for the study of Sexual Attitudes and Lifestyles already suggested that, in general, female interviewers are preferred by both male and female respondents, although some men are also willing to talk to a male interviewer (Spencer et al. 1988). A recent study of the sexual experiences of young male sex offenders also found that respondents were significantly more comfortable with a female interviewer, but recommended that self-disclosure about sexual material may be facilitated when interviewers of both gender are available (Kaplan, Becker and Tenke 1991). In the light of these findings, the team of interviewers for the four pre-pilots consisted entirely of women, but in each case respondents were asked if they would prefer to talk to a man. As expected, none of the 127 people interviewed requested a male interviewer. Thus for a large scale national survey we recommend that the majority of interviewers be women, but with some men included in the team. Respondents should be made aware that they can chose the gender of their interviewer if they have a particular preference.

In relation to ethnic background, the pre-pilots were unable to assess respondents' preferences because of the small number of people from ethnic minority backgrounds included in the study. Evidence from other studies is inconclusive, although some research suggests that interviewer characteristics such as gender and ethnic background may affect response, particularly where the subject of the study is directly linked to those characteristics or is pertinent to issues of gender or race (Schuman and Converse 1971; Kane and Macaulay 1993). However, little or no effect can be detected where the subject of the study is unrelated to these issues. On balance, it is likely that interviewer characteristics are not the major issue, but that interviewing skills and experience are of more significance in maximising the level and quality of response for a study of this kind (Fowler and Mangione 1990). A full-scale pilot could investigate these issues further.

Confidentiality and ethics

Because of the complex and sensitive nature of the subject under study, a number of measures were taken during the development work to ensure confidentiality and anonymity for respondents, and to address the question of the ethics of conducting a survey into the subject of child sexual abuse.

Preserving the anonymity of respondents

Confidentiality and anonymity are a feature of all SCPR surveys, and measures are routinely taken to safeguard these. Measures include, for example, using only serial numbers to identify questionnaires, and having separate documentation for recording respondents' names and addresses. In addition to this, standard SCPR procedures also ensure that possible identifiers are not added to questionnaires at a later date, and that subsequent analysis and reporting do not allow the identification of individual respondents. A similar system was used for the four pre-pilot studies, but with the additional precaution that Address Record Forms were kept under lock and key by the project researchers. Similar procedures were followed during the early development stage, where tape recordings and transcripts of unstructured interviews were identified only by a code number, and locked away with access restricted to members of the research team.

Apart from these measures for handling and storing data, respondents were given strict assurances about confidentiality both during the introduction at the time they consented to being interviewed, and in the covering explanatory letter. It may be, however, that further re-assurances could be given, for example in the form of a follow-up letter re-stating the confidentiality of respondents' identity and personal data.

Privacy during the interview itself

As discussed in Section 6, careful consideration was given during the feasibility study to the importance of ensuring privacy for the conduct of the interview itself. General population surveys tend to be carried out in people's own homes for reasons of convenience and cost, but also in order to put respondents at ease in the context of familiar surroundings. In some cases, however, this can pose problems for the confidentiality and privacy of the interview. Living conditions may make it hard to find a separate and private place for the interview to be carried out; and other household members, such as partners, parents, children, or friends may wish to be present during the interview. In all studies interviewers endeavour to interview the respondent alone, but this is not always possible. For the feasibility study, however, privacy was considered essential not only to ensure the quality of the data as discussed in Section 6, but because of ethical considerations. Interviewers were instructed to follow one of two courses where achieving privacy was a problem. In the first place they could book a time to return when the respondent could be on their own, or secondly they could offer an alternative venue.

In practice, during the pre-pilot studies, interviewers were usually able to arrange an alternative appointment, and other venues were not required. There were some cases, however, where privacy could not be negotiated because a husband or wife was keen to be present, and respondents were adamant that they "had no secrets" from their partner. Where interviews took place with another party to be present, interviewers reported finding it harder to establish rapport, but did not necessarily feel that a respondent was withholding important information. Whether or not the presence of a partner influences the type or detail of information given is difficult to establish, however, as it may be that only those with little to tell feel comfortable about giving an interview in front of someone else. Clearly, it would be important to attempt to achieve complete privacy for interviews in the national study, and this issue would need careful consideration during a large scale pilot study. For example, achieving privacy may prove particularly difficult in the case of young people still living in the parental home, and could have implications for the design and composition of the sample. (See Section 4).

Ethical considerations : the impact on respondents

Of all the ethical considerations associated with a study of child sexual abuse, the most important of all concerns the effects of the interview on survivors of childhood abuse. Even though the line of questioning adopted may be sensitive, containing no reference to "abuse" *per se*, and the format of the questions may be such that respondents are not asked to describe events in their own words, (see Section 5), nevertheless, the interview may well trigger painful and traumatic memories.

The impact of the interview process was given careful and thorough attention throughout the entire feasibility study. In the first place, as discussed in Section 5, every effort was made to present the interview in an open and non-judgemental light, and to make it as easy as possible for respondents to answer without explicit reference to particular behaviours. Secondly, inter-viewers were thoroughly trained to ensure that they could maintain a professional, neutral, but sympathetic stance during the course of the interview, putting respondents at their ease, and offering no hint or suggestion of appraisal.

Thirdly, serious consideration was given to the need for post-interview support for respondents who might have found the interview distressing, or who might have become upset at a later stage as a result of further memories being recalled. For each of the pre-pilot studies a list of local counselling and support services in the area was drawn up in consultation with SCOSAC, and left with respondents at the end of the interview.[1] In first two pre-pilots respondents were asked if they would like to have a list of local services, but this was later abandoned as it could sometimes create an awkward atmosphere, implying that respondents might themselves 'need help'. Later pre-pilots adopted a procedure of leaving the information with all respondents as a routine part of the study documentation.[2] The lists used are included in the Technical Appendix to this report.

In addition to the measures described above, the feasibility study attempted to find out how respondents had felt about the study as a whole, and about the more explicit questions regarding childhood sexual experiences. To this end, respondents were given opportunities to indicate the extent to which they had found the interview upsetting, embarrassing or shocking, and to comment on the value of the study as a whole. A feedback module at the end of the questionnaire explicitly probed for this kind of information, and a pre-paid reply slip was also left with respondents in case they wished to make separate comments at a later stage. These twin approaches allowed us to capture both immediate and longer term responses to the study. In general, it is fair to report that reactions were generally positive and favourable. Even where respondents had been somewhat surprised or embarrassed, they nevertheless appreciated the overall purpose and value of the study.[3] For example, one respondent wrote:

---

[1] The availability and comprehensiveness of counselling and support services throughout the country is a serious concern for this study. A large scale survey would have considerable resource implications as it is doubtful that the existing services would be sufficient to cope with a major increase in demand.

[2] With the second procedure, interviewers reported cases where respondents welcomed the information as potentially helpful for "someone they knew", but where the interviewer considered that the respondents might in fact make use of the lists themselves. Providing such as information as a matter of course removed any onus on the part of the respondent to make a special request, and allowed for the possibility that people might become upset some time after the interview had taken place, even where they were not aware of distress at the time. Follow-up interviews indicated that the provision of information about local services was appreciated and taken as a sign of responsible research practice.

[3] Some respondents also claimed that they had anticipated feeling awkward or embarrassed when agreeing to take part in the study, but in practice had found the experience "easier than expected". This confirms findings from the development work carried out for the National Survey of Sexual Attitudes and Lifestyles (Spencer et al 1988).

I have found this interview very interesting. I hope it will be useful to the researchers. In my view, openness and honesty about sex, sexuality and emotions are a positive and healthy way to conduct one's life.

Another commented:

It was interesting. It's important subject matter to research.

Disclosure of information about possible criminal activity

Finally, a review of ethical issues must also draw attention to the fact that during the course of an interview about childhood sexual experiences, respondents are asked a number of questions about the other people involved. This disclosure of information about third parties is particularly sensitive in the case of child sexual abuse because it may reveal cases of criminal activity. In many cases this may refer to past events and untraceable perpetrators, but it is possible that some information may be given about ongoing abuse or traceable perpetrators. Furthermore, a study may reveal information about respondents' own sexual contacts in adulthood with minors; indeed, in the feasibility study we asked about this directly in the self-completed supplement in Module 9. Although reporting of known child abuse cases is obligatory in the United States unless researchers have applied for special exemption, a system of mandatory reporting does not exist in this country. The research team gave a great deal of consideration to this issue, and concluded that professional research ethics must be respected, and that guarantees of confidentiality must in all cases be upheld. The alternative procedure of withdrawing assurances of confidentiality, or of notifying respondents that evidence of current perpetration would be reported is in our view unjustifiable in the context of a large national survey, and would in any case jeopardise the reliability of the findings.

Section Ten Conclusions and Recommendations

This final section summarises the findings of the feasibility study in relation to a number of technical, procedural and ethical issues, and outlines the implications for a national survey of the prevalence of child sexual abuse in this country. Existing data on the prevalence of abuse in Britain provide some indications of the scale of the problem, but are severely limited in their scope and generalisability by virtue of their sample sizes and methods, and their approach to defining the issue. The feasibility study has, therefore, worked to develop a methodology for a national survey which would overcome these shortcomings, provide robust data for the population as a whole, and which would considerably expand the existing knowledge base in this country. We believe that a technically rigorous, large scale national survey of the prevalence of child sexual abuse is certainly feasible, can achieve respectable response rates, and can provide new and valuable data. Such data would both enhance understanding of the problem of abuse, and assist with the planning of a range of health, education, and social services.

Throughout the feasibility study we took the view that a study of prevalence alone, without supporting contextual information, would be both substantively and technically inadequate to achieve the aims outlined above. Substantively, we have argued that abuse cannot be understood without reference to the context within which it takes place. Contextual information needed might include for example: the broad range of childhood sexual experiences in the population at large, levels of sexual knowledge and formal sex education, the circumstances and effects of different types of experiences, the extent to which those experiences are reported or discovered, and the influence of different kinds of family circumstances and relationships. Technically, we have shown that the collection of high quality data on sexual experiences, and particularly sexually traumatic experiences, also requires careful attention to context and approach in order to present questions in a sensitive and ethically acceptable way and to maximise participation. A national survey should, therefore, aim to provide two levels of data: firstly an overall estimate of the proportion of adults in the general population who have experienced various forms of sexual abuse during their childhood, and secondly information pertaining to the broad context within which child sexual abuse takes place.

Approach and Presentation

Perhaps the first issue to require resolution in the feasibility study was that of how best to approach the public in a survey of this kind, and how to present the study. As we have discussed, the need to maximise participation in a sensitive survey may not necessarily be compatible with ethical research practice. Oblique approaches, whereby a small number of questions about sexual abuse are bedded in a broader and apparently unrelated topic, were evaluated and subsequently rejected on both technical and ethical grounds: they allow insufficient opportunity for asking about the circumstances and effects of abuse, and do not adequately or honestly prepare the respondent. Direct references to "abuse", on the other hand, were found to have the disadvantages of possibly offending or deterring respondents. By making the focus of the study on "sexual experiences before the age of 16", it was possible to devise a presentation context for the study which openly and honestly reflected the subject matter, and referred quite directly both to "childhood" and to "sex". Given that this approach still retained a 'sensitive' quality which could jeopardise overall response, interviewers were required to make particular efforts to overcome this, and, as response rates in pre-pilot four demonstrate, appeared largely to have succeeded in this. In devising a method of approach to the public, we therefore recommend that a national survey:

- adopt a *direct* approach to the extent that sexual experiences in childhood are explicitly referred to

- adopt an *indirect* approach to the extent that overt references to abuse or victimisation are avoided

- undertake thorough interviewer training and briefing in the specific skills required to recruit respondents to the survey

Response

The issue of response is, of course, closely linked to that of approach and presentation. The problem of poor overall response rates in a survey of this kind has undermined the reliability of the data produced by much previous research, and the feasibility study set out to evaluate the nature of this problem and to find ways of overcoming it. Our findings suggest that despite the sensitivity of the subject matter, given careful attention to procedure there is no reason to doubt that the general public can be induced to take part in such a survey, and that they can be recruited in sufficient numbers to provide acceptable overall response rates. For example, the careful development and refinement of our initial method of presentation of the study to respondents enabled us to achieve a 71% response rate by the fourth pre-pilot. In terms of demographic characteristics a good range of respondents was achieved, although the small sample sizes to date mean that a full scale pilot would be required to fully evaluate related issues such as potential bias in the sample. The response rate achieved by the final pre-pilot compares favourably with other surveys of sexual matters generally and with previous studies of child sexual abuse.

Related to the issue of overall response is that of item response; that is, the propensity of respondents to refuse to answer certain questions within the interview. Again, poor item response in some previous studies has resulted in data sets which lack overall reliability in terms of prevalence rates. In the feasibility study, the gradual, modular design of the questionnaire, with a sensitive introduction to the subject of sexual experience in childhood, achieved a 100% item response rate across the four pre-pilots. It was found that a combination of sensitively worded questions, permission-seeking when probing, and careful attention to interviewer technique encouraged rapport between respondent and interviewer which was highly conducive to the disclosure of even the most painful and socially stigmatised experiences.

With regard to the issue of maximising response, our recommendations can be summarised as follows:

- to maximise *overall* response: pay careful attention to the method of approach and presentation (see above) and to interviewer training

- to maximise *item* response: consider as a priority the need to maintain respondent comfort and co-operation within the interview at all times, and incorporate measures to promote this in questionnaire structure, question wording and interviewing technique

Questionnaire

In designing a structured data collection instrument, two somewhat different requirements informed our thinking. One was the need for a technically flexible questionnaire in order to capture the complex nature of certain aspects of childhood sexual experiences, which may undergo many changes over time. The other was the need for sensitive ordering and wording of questions in order to promote a full and frank response. An open and flexible strategy was therefore pursued during development of the structure and design of a questionnaire. Respondents were taken carefully and gradually from background questions about their childhood, family circumstances and relationships, through the period of their sexual development and how they "learned about sex", to more explicit questions about the nature of their early sexual experiences. These questions were set within the normative context of "growing up", and enabled respondents themselves to define the nature of their encounters from mutual sexual exploration through to victimising and abusive experiences. Show cards were used to help ease potential embarrassment or difficulty when identifying the precise content of sexual experience.

This overall strategy and approach to surveying child sexual abuse was found to have a number of distinct advantages. Firstly by adopting a neutral and open focus it provides a benchmark for the range and diversity of sexual experience prior to the age of 16. Secondly, by asking a wide range of contextual questions, it allows for different kinds of definitions of child sexual abuse to be assessed and compared, and can provide estimates of prevalence accordingly. Thirdly, it can encompass both 'subjective' and 'objective' definitions, taking account of respondents' perspectives, as well as cultural, clinical, or legal considerations. Fourthly, by using such methods as show cards a high level of detail regarding sexual experiences, previously only possible in clinical studies where interviewers are specialists in the field, can be achieved. Finally, the study includes sexual experiences between same-age peers as well as between adults and children, and permits analysis to be undertaken as to the prevalence and effects of this type of abuse. In designing and developing a structured questionnaire to be used in a general population survey, we would therefore advocate:

- a modular structure, moving respondents gradually from contextual to more explicit questions

- a flexible instrument for recording the diversity and complexity of childhood sexual experiences

- the use of show cards for eliciting detail on the content of sexual activities

Case Definition

Two issues dominate the debate on definitions of "child sexual abuse"; one theoretical and one technical. The first is the requirement for new studies to maintain comparability with existing ones, and the other is the need to maximise participation and reporting to obtain as close an estimate as possible to the "true" rate of prevalence in the population. To this end, it is our contention that in attempting to survey child sexual abuse in this country, there are a number of advantages to be gained from adopting an inclusive and *post hoc* approach to the issue of definition. Rather than defining child sexual abuse at the outset, thereby limiting the scope and type of information collected, we opted for a strategy of 'minimum definition but maximum information'. In practice this was implemented by focusing on sexual experiences of *any* kind under the age of 16, but with a wide range of questions to determine the age of the participants, the nature of the relationship and content of the sexual activity, the extent of willingness or mutuality involved, overall feelings and perceptions about the encounter, and immediate and longer-term effects. Specific examples of the broad range of experiences which might be included were also provided by means of detailed show cards, in order to encourage respondents themselves to define sexual experience in the broadest possible terms. This approach makes possible the evaluation of childhood sexual experiences in a number of different ways, according to a variety of different conceptualizations of abuse, and to compare findings with other studies by varying the units of analysis. Our recommendations in respect of case definition would therefore be:

- to promote maximal reporting by avoidance of pre-definition of the experiences under investigation, or otherwise attaching value labels to experiences

- to apply *post hoc* definitions of different types of childhood sexual experiences in order to permit analytic comparison with other studies

Sample

Previous studies of prevalence have been limited in their power of generalisation both by virtue of their use of non-random samples as well as their often relatively small overall sample size.

One of the priorities of the feasibility study was to assess the sampling requirements for a large scale national survey based on statistically sound, probability sampling methods. The selection of an appropriate sampling frame was a key consideration in this case. The small users Postcode Address File (PAF) was used to generate samples of addresses in two of the four pilot studies, in combination with random selection of individuals within addresses carried out by the interviewer. This method is regularly used in other large scale surveys of the general population and is considered to be the most appropriate one for sampling the major proportion of respondents in a national survey of the prevalence of child sexual abuse. However, there is evidence to suggest that certain special populations who are not generally covered by standard survey sampling frames, such as the homeless and those resident in institutions, may have elevated rates of sexual abuse in childhood. Thus it may be particularly important not to exclude such people from a national survey of prevalence. To this end, we advise that supplementary frames to PAF be considered, and alternative sampling methods be used to access these groups.

In terms of sample size, we have indicated that this will be conditioned by the level at which data analysis is desired to take place. Broadly speaking, the finer the level of analytical detail required, the greater the overall sample size will need to be. Because of the comparatively low base rate of child sexual abuse, and particularly of certain forms of abuse, a substantial overall sample size would be required in order to generate sufficient cases for quantitative analysis. Because previous estimates of prevalence have varied so widely, it is difficult, in advance of a full scale pilot, to predict the precise size of sample that would be required; however, our recommendation at this stage would be for as large a sample as resources permit. A sample of the order of the National Survey of Sexual Attitudes and Lifestyles recently carried out by SCPR on behalf of the Wellcome Trust (19,000 achieved interviews) might be a suitable comparison.

The structure and composition of a national sample is also an important consideration. On the question of age, for example, for the purposes of the feasibility study ages ranged from 18 to 60, but it may be that a narrower age band would be preferable. Certainly among the younger age groups it is often the case that young people are still living in their family home, which could raise practical issues about the privacy and confidentiality of interviews, or ethical issues in that a young person might still be living with an abuser. There are also issues related to cultural background which remain to be resolved; for example, whether the survey would include adults not brought up in this country, or would focus only on abuse of children which had occurred within Britain itself. Before a national survey could be launched it would be important for a full scale pilot study to be undertaken in order to finalise these and other aspects of the design and composition of the sample. At this stage, however, we would recommend the following:

- a PAF sample with random selection of individuals at household level for the bulk of the sample

- supplementary sampling frames and sampling methods for special population groups such as the homeless or those resident in institutions

- a large overall sample size to yield sufficient cases to enable analysis of rarer sub-groups

- further consideration to be given to the question of respondents' age and childhood background in respect of the country in which they were brought up in

Fieldwork

Evaluation of the research literature and experimentation with different modes of administration have led us to conclude that, as a main mode of administration, face-to-face interviews hold a number of advantages for a survey on a sensitive issue such as child sexual abuse. They allow for a more complex and flexible approach to questioning, and we believe are most suited to obtaining good estimates of prevalence rates where rapport can be established between interviewer and respondent. In order to achieve these advantages, however, it is essential that interviewers be well prepared and trained. Throughout the feasibility study attention was paid to these needs, and we advocate rigorous training and briefing of interviewers before they are sent out into the field on a survey such as this. Procedures adopted to develop a training programme included: provision of a full training day devised and carried out in conjunction with a specialist agency (SCOSAC); full face-to-face briefing procedures for each new pre-pilot; evaluation and monitoring of interviewer performance through audio-taped interviews; full de-briefing for interviewers after each wave of interviewing; and ongoing availability of support for field staff throughout the study.

Certain other practical issues also loomed large in the feasibility study which would impact on fieldwork organisation in a national survey; principally on the length of fieldwork periods needed. The need for privacy to conduct interviews, and the difficulty of obtaining such privacy in some households pointed to the need for extended fieldwork periods to allow for re-scheduling of appointments where necessary, or the provision of alternative local interviewing venues. Although the response rate achieved by the final pre-pilot was respectable, we would also advocate re-issuing refusals where possible to boost overall response; and offering respondents a choice of interviewer gender. This would also extend fieldwork periods. Finally, because of the challenging nature of recruiting and interviewing in a survey on this subject, we feel that experienced and known interviewers are best suited to this work. Large scale recruitment of new field workers is not, therefore, advised.

For a national survey our recommendations are therefore to:

- carry out full training and briefing for interviewers to familiarize them with the subject matter and prepare them thoroughly for the challenging nature of interviewing in this field

- allow for extended fieldwork periods to circumvent the problem of privacy for interviewing

- consider further the possibility of providing alternative local venues for some interviews

- provide for flexible deployment of interviewers so that respondents can be given a choice of interviewer gender

- use experienced and known interviewers wherever possible

Memory and recall

All studies which rely heavily on retrospective data are subject to possible failures and distortions of recall. In the feasibility study the pre-school period was found to be especially hard for some respondents to recall, and that in general questioning had to focus carefully on techniques for the contextual location, and hence chronological positioning of memories. A further problem in child abuse research particularly is the phenomenon of blocking: that is, the tendency for unpleasant or traumatic memories to be suppressed or buried as a form of psychological coping mechanism. Although a certain proportion of such memories will never be recovered in a survey even by sensitive questioning, there is evidence that a survey interview may trigger memories of childhood sexual experiences, but that some of these may not surface until after the interview itself is over. We have, therefore, argued that a second phase of data collection in the form of a follow-up interview (either face-to-face or perhaps by postal self-completion questionnaire) might prove indispensable. Such interviews would not necessarily have to be carried out with the entire sample, but should be attempted with some proportion of respondents in order to assess the accuracy of prevalence rates gained through an initial interview. In summary, we advise:

- careful attention to questioning techniques to help stimulate memory
- a follow-up phase of data collection to maximise reporting of childhood sexual experiences which may initially have been suppressed or blocked

Finally there may be issues of over-reporting of sexual abuse due to the so-called 'false memory syndrome'. Although there is no evidence that this problem is widespread, and we do not consider it a serious threat to the integrity of prevalence estimates from a community survey such as the one proposed here, the incorporation of questions designed to probe the 'origin' of memories of abuse may be indicated where the respondent reports only having recovered memories in adulthood.

Ethics

A major concern to be addressed in the feasibility study was that of the ethics of conducting a national survey on this subject and the preparation that would be required to ensure that neither respondents nor interviewers would be adversely affected as a result of taking part.

With regard to the effects of the study on interviewers, we took care during training and briefing, as described above, to familiarise interviewers with the subject of child sexual abuse to ensure that they could establish rapport, carry out an interview in a professional but sympathetic manner, and be able to cope with any disturbing material they might encounter.

On the question of the impact of the study on respondents, careful attention was paid to respondent sensibilities. Firstly, the subject was introduced in a neutral, non-judgemental fashion, and permission sought at each "change of gear" in the questionnaire. Secondly, respondents were given the opportunity to comment on the study and to express their views about taking part at the end of the interview. As well as providing important methodological information for the research team, this proved an effective way of acknowledging the sensitive and potentially controversial nature of the study.

Thirdly, with regard to the issue of confidentiality, we found that some respondents expressed a desire for extra reassurances after the interviewer had left. It must not be forgotten that some respondents will reveal very sensitive and personal information in interviews that they have never before disclosed to anyone, and may feel vulnerable after the interview because of this. Finally, each respondent was given a list of local counselling services and help lines in their area. Feedback from those who took part in the feasibility study suggested that these measures were greatly appreciated by respondents, and reactions were overwhelmingly favourable to the value of the study overall. Should a large scale survey be undertaken, however, careful consideration would need to be given to the comprehensiveness of lists, the best way of presenting information and facilitating contact between respondents in need and such services, and of course the capacity of existing counselling services to cope with the increase in demand which such a survey would be expected to generate. It may be that a specially created national help line, which could refer callers on to local services, would be the best way of operationalising support for respondents in the survey. Our recommendations, then, for a large scale national study in this regard are as follows:

- lists of local support services be provided to all respondents
- support services be briefed on the existence of the survey and consideration be given on how best to assist them to cope with increased demands on resources if necessary
- respondents be given the opportunity and encouragement to comment on the interview process in general, and on sections of the questionnaire in particular
- a post-interview letter be sent to all respondents thanking them for their help, reaffirming the principle of confidentiality and procedures taken to maintain this. This letter could perhaps also urge respondents to contact local services or a special help line if the interview has raised any personal issues which they would like to discuss further
- a full familiarisation and support programme be provided to all interviewers working on the survey

Implications for the future

In summary, we conclude that it would certainly be possible to carry out a national survey of the prevalence of child sexual abuse. Although we recommend that a large pilot be carried out to further illuminate some of the technical issues, such as sample size, sample composition and possible sources of response bias, as a result of the development work described in this report, we have been able to arrive at the following:

- a method of approach to the public and presentation of such a survey which is both ethically satisfactory and technically conducive to good response rates

- a presentation context for questioning which facilitates the recall and disclosure of sensitive material

- a structured questionnaire of sufficient flexibility to capture the range and diversity of childhood sexual experiences, both positive and negative, both normal and abusive

- an approach to case definition which maximises reporting, permits analytic comparison with previous research definitions, and takes account of respondents' perspectives as well as cultural, clinical and legal considerations

- a survey methodology which we believe can provide robust national estimates of the prevalence of child sexual abuse, combined with levels of detail about the nature, circumstances and content of abuse that have previously only been available to clinical researchers

- a survey methodology which provides information on child sexual abuse within the context of the *full* range of childhood sexual experiences, thus considerably adding to the current knowledge base, and to the debate on abuse.

References

BADGELY R., ALLARD H., McCORMOCK N., PROUDFOOT P., FORTIN D., RAE-GRANT Q., GELINAS P., PEPIN L., and SUTHERLAND S. [Committee on sexual offences against children and youth] (1984) *Sexual offences against children.* Ottawa: Canadian Government Publishing Centre.

BAKER T. (1983) Sexual abuse within the family. *19 Magazine* **April** 35–40

BAKER A. and DUNCAN S. (1985) Child sexual abuse : a study of prevalence in Great Britain. *Child Abuse and Neglect* **9** 457–467

BARTON J.A. (1958) Asking the embarrassing question. *Public Opinion Quarterly* **22** 67–68

BASS E. and DAVIS L. (1990) *The courage to heal—A guide for women survivors of child sexual abuse.* London: Cedar.

BECK A.T., WARD C.H., MENDELSON M., MACK J. and ERBAUGH J. (1961) An inventory for measuring depression. *Archives of General Psychiatry* **4** 561–571

BEITCHMAN J., ZUCKER K., HOOD J., DA COSTA G., ALIMAN D., and CASAVIA E. A review of the long term effects of child sexual abuse. *Child Abuse and Neglect* **16** 101–118

BELL A. and WEINBERG M. (1981) *Sexual preference: its development among men and women.* Bloomington: Indiana University Press

BERLINER L. and CONTE J.R. (1990) The process of victimization: the victim's perspective. *Child Abuse and Neglect* **14** 29–40

BERGER A.M., KNUTSON J.F., MEHM J.G. and PERKING K.A. (1988) The self-report of punitive childhood experiences of young adults and adolescents. *Child Abuse and Neglect* **12** 251–262

BLUME E.S. (1985) *Secret survivors: uncovering incest and its after effects in women.* New York: Ballantine

BOLTON F.G.. MORRIS L.A. and MacEACHRON A.E. (1989) *Males at risk: the other side of child sexual abuse.* California: Sage Publications

BRIERE J. and RUNTZ M. (1987) A brief measure of victimization effects: The Trauma Symptom Checklist (TSC-33) [Paper presented at the Third National Family Violence Research Conference, Durham, NH]

BRIERE J. and RUNTZ M. (1988) Symptomatology associated with childhood sexual victimization in a non-clinical adult sample. *Child Abuse and Neglect* **12** 51–59

BROOKE L. (1977) Postal survey procedures, in Hoinville G. and Jowell R. (eds) *Survey research practice*. Aldershot: Gower

BROWNE A., and FINKELHOR D (1986) The impact of child sexual abuse: a review of the research. *Psychological Bulletin* **99:1**

BUTLER-SLOSS LADY JUSTICE E. (1988) *Report of the inquiry into child abuse in Cleveland 1987*. London: HMSO

CHERRY C. (1991) Male sexual abuse—what's happening in the USA? *Off Centre Annual Review* **1990–91** Off Centre, 25 Hackney Grove, London E8 3NR

CIBA Foundation (1984) *Child abuse within the family*. London: Tavistock

CONTE J.R. (1985) The effects of sexual abuse on children: a critique and suggestions for future research. *Victimology* **10** 110–130

CONTE J.R. and SCHUERMAN J.R. (1987) The effects of sexual abuse on children: a multi-dimensional view. *Journal of Interpersonal Violence* **2** 380–390

DEGENER T. (1992) The right to be different: implications for child protection. *Child Abuse Review* **1** 151–155

DEROGATIS L., LIPMAN R.S., RICHELS K., ULENHUTH E.H. and COVI L. (1974) The Hopkins Symptom Checklist (HSCL): a self-report symptom inventory. *Behavioural Science* **19** 1–15

EVERTSZ J.C. (1992) Beyond figures: offending behaviour in child molesters. Unpublished paper, kindly provided by the Gracewell Institute, Birmingham.

FINKELHOR D. (1979) *Sexually victimized children*. New York: Free Press

FINKELHOR D. (1984) *Child sexual abuse: new theory and research*. New York: Free Press

FINKELHOR D. (1986) *A sourcebook on child sexual abuse*. Beverley Hills: Sage

FINKELHOR D., HOTALING G., LEWIS I.A. and SMITH C. (1990) Sexual abuse in a national survey of adult men and women: prevalence, character-istics, and risk factors. *Child Abuse and Neglect* **14:1** 19–28

FOWLER F.J. and MANGIONE T.W. (1990) *Minimising interviewer-related error.* Applied Social Research Methods Series **18** California: Sage

FRIEDRICH W.N. (1988) Child abuse and sex abuse, in Green R.L. (ed) *The MMPI: use in specific diagnostic groups*. New York: Grune and Stratton

FRIEDRICH W.N., URQUIZA A.J. and BEILKE R.L. (1986) Behaviour problems in sexually abused young children. *Journal of Paediatric Psychology* **11** 47–57

FRITZ G.S., STOLL K. and WAGNER N.A. (1981) A comparison of males and females who were sexually molested as children. *Journal of Sex and Marital Therapy* **7** 54–59

FROMUTH M. (1983) *The long term psychological impact of childhood sexual abuse.* Unpublished doctoral dissertation, Auburn University

FROMUTH M. and BURKHART B. (1987) Childhood sexual victimization among college men: definitional and methodological issues. *Violence and Victims* **2:4** 241–253

GOLDBERG D. (1972) *The Detection of Psychiatric Illness by Questionnaire.* London: Oxford University Press

GROTH A.N. and BURGESS A.W. (1979) Sexual trauma in the life histories of rapists and child molesters. *Victimology* **4** 10–16

HALES J. (1992) *British Crime Survey 1992: technical report.* London: SCPR.

HAMILTON G.V. (1929) *A research in marriage.* New York: Albert and Charles Boni

HAUGAARD J. and REPUCCI N.J. (1988) *The sexual abuse of children.* San Francisco: Josey-Bass

HAUGAARD J. and EMERY R. (1989) Methodological issues in child abuse research. *Child Abuse and Neglect.* **13** 89–100

Health Education Authority and the Sports Council (1992) *Report on the Allied-Dunbar Fitness Survey : main findings*

HELMRICH R. and STAPP J. (1974) Short forms of the Texas Social Behaviour Inventory (TSBI), an objective measure of self-esteem. *Bulletin Psychonomic Society* **4 (SA)** 473–475

HERMAN J.L. and SCHATCOW E. (1986 May) Verification of memories of childhood sexual trauma. [Paper presented to the annual meeting of the American Psychiatric Association, Washington D.C.]

HERZBERGER S.D. (1993) The cyclical pattern of child abuse: a study of research methodology, in Renzetti C. and Lee R. (eds) *Researching sensitive topics.* California: Sage

HOLMES T.H. and RAHE R.H. (1967) The Social Re-adjustment Rating Scale. *Journal of Psychosomatic Research* **11** 213–218

JOHNSON A.M., WADSWORTH J., WELLINGS K., BRADSHAW S. and FIELD J. (1992) Sexual lifestyles and HIV risk. *Nature* **360** 410–412

JOHNSON A.M., WADSWORTH J., WELLINGS K., BRADSHAW S. and FIELD J. (1994) *Sexual Attitudes and Lifestyles.* Oxford: Blackwell Scientific Press

KANE E.W. and MACAULAY L.J. (1993) Interviewer gender and gender attitudes. *Public Opinion Quarterly* **57** 1–28

KAPLAN M., BECKER J. and TENKE C. (1991) Influence of abuse history on male adolescent self-reported comfort with interviewer gender. *Journal of Interpersonal Violence* **6:1** 3–11.

KELLY L., REAGAN L., and BURTON S. (1991) *An exploratory study of the prevalence of sexual abuse in a sample of 16–21 year olds.* End of award report to the Economic and Social Research Council. Child Abuse Studies Unit, University of North London.

KELLY L., REAGAN L., and BURTON S. (1991a) *Initial findings and reflections on researching the prevalence of child sexual abuse.* Child Abuse Studies Unit, University North London

KELLY L. (1992) The connections between disability and child abuse: a review of the research evidence. *Child Abuse Review* **1** 157–167

KEMPE R.S. and KEMPE C.H. (1978) *Child Abuse.* Glasgow: Fontana

KERCHER G. and McSHANE M. (1984) The prevalence of child sexual abuse victimisation in an adult sample of Texan residents. *Child Abuse and Neglect* **8** 495–502

KINSEY A.C., POMEROY W.B., MARTIN C.E. and GEBHARD P.H. (1953) *Sexual behaviour in the human female.* Philadelphia: W.B. Saunders

KOSHAL N. (1986) *An audience analysis on "Childwatch".* BBC Broadcasting Research, Information section, unpublished.

KNUTSON J. and SELNER N. (1994) Punitive childhood experiences reported by young adults over a 10-year period. *Child Abuse and Neglect* **18** 155–166

LANDIS J. (1956) Experiences of 500 children with adult sexual deviants. *Psychiatric Quarterly Supplement* **30** 91–109

LA FONTAINE J. (1990) *Child Sexual Abuse.* Cambridge: Polity

LEWIS I.A. (1985) [Los Angeles Times Poll No. 98] Unpublished raw data

LYNN P. (1992) *The survey of single homeless people: technical report.* London: SCPR

LYNN P. and LIEVESLEY D. (1991) *Drawing general population samples in Great Britain.* London: SCPR

MARTIN J., ANDERSON J,. ROMANS S., MULLEN P. and O'SHEA M. (1993) Asking about child sexual abuse: methodological implications of a 2-stage survey. *Child Abuse and Neglect* **17** 383–392

MATHEWS R., MATTHEWS J.K. and SPELTZ K. (1989) *Female Sexual Offenders: an exploratory study.* Vermont: Safer Society Press

MOSER C.A. and KALTON G. (1971) *Survey methods in social investigation.* Aldershot: Gower

NASH C.L. and WEST D.J. (1985) Sexual molestation of young girls: a retrospective study, in West D.J. (Ed) *Sexual victimisation*. Aldershot: Gower

PETERS J.J. (1976) Children who are victims of sexual assault and the psychology of offenders. *American Journal of Psychotherapy* **30:3** 395–421

RAUSCH K. and KNUTSON J.F. (1991) Self-report of punitive childhood experiences and those of siblings. *Child Abuse and Neglect* **15** 29–36

RISIN L. and KOSS M. (1987) The sexual abuse of boys: prevalence and descriptive characteristics of childhood victimisations. *Journal of Interpersonal Violence* **2:3** 309–323

Royal Belfast Hospital and Queen's University (1990) *Child Sexual Abuse in Northern Ireland*. Antrim: Greystoke

RUSH F. (1980) *The Best-Kept Secret: sexual abuse of children*. Florida: McGraw-Hill

RUSSELL D.E.H. (1984) *Sexual Exploitation: rape, child sexual abuse and workplace harassment*. California: Sage

SCHUMAN H. and CONVERSE J.M. (1971) The effects of black and white interviewers on black responses in 1968. *Public Opinion Quarterly* **35** 44–68

SEIDNER A.L. and CALHOUN K.S. (1984) Childhood sexual abuse: factors related to differential adjustment. [Paper presented to the Second National Conference for Family Violence Researchers, Durham, N.H.]

SIEGAL J., SORENSON S., GOLDING J., BURNHAM A. and STEIN J. (1987) The prevalence of childhood sexual assault: the Los Angeles Epidemiological Area project. *American Journal of Epidemiology* **1266** 1141–1153

SINGER M., HUSSEY D. and STOM K.J. (1992) Grooming the victim: an analysis of a perpetrator's seduction letter. *Child Abuse and Neglect* **16** 877–886

SPENCER L., FAULKNER A. and KEEGAN J. (1988) *Talking about sex: asking the public about sexual behaviour and attitudes* London: SCPR

SUMMIT R.C. (1983) The child sexual abuse accommodation syndrome. *Child Abuse and Neglect* 7 177–193

VIZARD E. (1989) Incidence and prevalence of child sexual abuse, in Ouston J. (Ed) *The consequences of child sexual abuse*. Association for child psychology and psychiatry, Occasional Papers No. 3

WALTERS D.R. (1975) *Physical and sexual abuse of children: causes and treatment*. Bloomington: Indiana University Press

WIDOM C.S. (1988) Sampling biases and implications for child abuse research. *American Journal of Orthopsychiatry* **58(2)** April 1988

Women's Research Centre (1989) *Recollecting our lives: women's experience of child sexual abuse*. Vancouver: Press Gang

WYATT G.E. (1985) The sexual abuse of Afro-American and White American women in childhood. *Child Abuse and Neglect* **9** 507–519

WYATT G.E. and PETERS S.D. (1986a) Issues in the definition of child sexual abuse. *Child Abuse and Neglect* **10** 231–240

WYATT G.E. and PETERS S.D. (1986b) Methodological considerations in research on the prevalence of child sexual abuse. *Child Abuse and Neglect* **10** 241–251

The prevalence of child sexual abuse in Britain: a feasibility study for a large scale national survey of the general population

TECHNICAL APPENDIX

Deborah Ghate
Liz Spencer
1994

P5214/1217

Contents

Technical Appendix

Design and Conduct of the Study: overview

Because of the challenging and sensitive nature of this study, we adopted a developmental, incremental approach in which each new stage built upon the findings of the last. A great strength was our ability to draw on both qualitative and quantitative research methods, and we moved from qualitative, to quantitative, and back again to qualitative methods as we explored the various issues arising during the course of the study. An initial familiarisation phase was followed by depth interviews with known survivors of child sexual abuse and with members of the general population. The substantive and methodological information gained from this phase informed the next stage of the study: semi-structured interviews with a quota sample of the general population. A second quota-sampled stage followed this, incorporating interviews with four survivors to test the questionnaire, and to form the basis of comparison with qualitative data. Two further pre-pilots were then carried out using random samples of the general population (drawn from the Postcodes Address File for small users within certain geographical areas) in order to develop a fully-structured questionnaire. Figure 1 summarises the overall design of the study.

Figure 1   **Design of the Feasibility Study**

Phase 1 : Familiarisation
- review of the literature
- consultations with clinicians and practitioners
- consultations with academics and researchers

Phase 2 : Qualitative Interviews
- group discussion with survivors
- depth interviews with survivors
- depth interviews with general population

Phase 3 : Developing a Structured Questionnaire
- pre-pilot 1 – semi-structured interviews
- pre-pilot 2 – semi-structured interviews
- pre-pilot 3 – structured interviews

Phase 4 : Fully Structured Interviews
- pre-pilot 4 – structured interviews
- depth follow-up interviews

A total of 25 qualitative depth interviews, and 127 survey interviews were completed over the course of four phases. Table 1 summarises the stages of fieldwork during the course of the study, including the sample type, numbers

Table 1. **Summary of fieldwork stages in the feasibility study**

Phase	Stage	Sample Type	Area	Number of interviews completed			Interviewers	Approach
				All	Women	Men		
2	Depth interviews	Networked: known survivors	London, Bedfordshire, Reading	13	9	4	Research team	Through professionals: *'a survey of child sexual abuse'*
2	Depth interviews	Quota: general population	Portsmouth, Bedfordshire	7	4	3	Research team	a) *'a survey of childhood and children's understanding of sex'* (4 interviews) b) *'a survey of childhood and family life'* (3 interviews)
3	Pre-pilot 1	Quota: general population	Bradford, Birmingham, Portsmouth, Newcastle	21	12	9	Field interviewers	*'a survey of childhood and children's understanding of sex'*
3	Pre-pilot 2	a) Quota: general population b) Networked: survivors	Bradford, Birmingham, Portsmouth, Newcastle, Essex, Plymouth, London, Reading	20 4	10 3	10 1	Field interviewers	*'a survey of childhood and children's understanding of sex'*
3	Pre-pilot 3	Random (PAF): General population	Essex, Birmingham, Bradford, Reading, London, Portsmouth	38	20	18	Field interviewers & Research team	a) *'a survey of childhood and children's knowledge and understanding of sex'* (29 interviews) b) *'a survey of public attitudes to child sexual abuse'* (9 interviews)
4	Pre-pilot 4	Random (PAF)*: General population *Simulated: checked against ER	Essex, Birmingham, Bradford, Reading, London, Portsmouth, Newcastle	48	27	21	Field interviewers & Research team	*'learning about sex: a survey of children's early knowledge and experience'*
4	Depth follow-up interviews	Selected from pre-pilot 4	Essex, London	5	3	2	Research team	For feedback purposes

of interviews achieved at each stage, the areas in which interviewing took place, and the different approaches which were used to recruit respondents to the sample.

Design and Conduct of the Study: the four phases

Phase One – Familiarisation

During this initial phase of the study we conducted a review of the literature on child sexual abuse, focusing both on substantive issues and on the methodological findings of other studies. Amongst other issues we reviewed the latest thinking on how and why child sexual abuse occurs, what is known about the characteristics of victims and perpetrators, and the long and short term effects of child sexual abuse. From a methodological standpoint we examined existing estimates of prevalence and associated statistics, and familiarised ourselves with the numerous definitions of child sexual abuse used by previous researchers. We examined interview schedules and questionnaires used in other studies, as well as the approaches used and the context in which questions on childhood sexual abuse were asked.

During this phase we also consulted widely with clinicians, practitioners and academics working in the field. Clinicians and practitioners were able to provide us with valuable insights from their experience with child victims, adult survivors and perpetrators of all ages, and advise on aspects of the study such as encouraging and dealing with disclosure, the range of sexual experiences in childhood which would be encountered, and the possible effects on survivors (and perpetrators) of participating in the study. With researchers who had carried out studies of the prevalence of sexual abuse we were able to discuss aspects of research methodology and obtain their views on issues such as context and approach, question wording and mode of administration. The purpose and content of Phase One are summarised below.

Phase One
Aim:

- to review substantive issues in child sexual abuse from professionals' perspectives
- to review methodological and technical issues for a prevalence study

Carried out:

- review of the literature
- consultations with clinicians and practitioners
- consultations with academics and researchers

Phase Two – Group Discussion and 20 Depth interviews

Talking to survivors

During this phase, as a first step, the members of the research team met with a group of seven men and women who were all users of a support group for adults who had been sexually abused as children, run by a Rape Crisis Centre. The group discussed aspects of the research and provided an opportunity for the research team to gain a preliminary insight into survivors' attitudes to a survey. This discussion was followed by depth interviews with survivors of child sexual abuse, some of whom had attended the group discussion, and some of whom were recruited through other sources. Nine women and four men were networked through counsellors and other professionals working in the field, using both personal contacts and an item in a SCOSAC[1] newsletter circulated to professionals. Practitioners were asked to inform any adult survivors they worked with that the research was taking place, and to pass on an information letter and contact number. Survivors then contacted a member of the research team direct to express interest in taking part in the study. All interviews in this phase were carried out by members of the research team; the interviews were extremely comprehensive and ranged in length from two to four hours. A wide range of sexual experiences were described by the group, from a single incident of childhood rape to prolonged abuse over many years by multiple perpetrators. Cases involving both male and female perpetrators were represented, and one case involving 'ritual' abuse was reported. Survivors interviewed ranged in age from 22 to 54.

Talking to the general population

Depth interviews with four women and three men from the general population were also carried out in Phase Two. Nothing was known in advance about the childhood sexual history of these respondents, who ranged in age from 22 to 48. Recruitment for the interviews was carried out in two areas by experienced SCPR field staff according to a simple quota based on sex, age and marital status, using two different methods of approach. The interviews were conducted by the research team. The interviews covered similar background information about childhood to that covered in the interviews with survivors, and explored early sexual knowledge and experiences. Phase Two is outlined below, and examples of relevant documents are given.

---

[1] Standing Committee on Sexually Abused Children, 73 St Charles Square, London W10 6EJ

Phase Two

Aim:

- to explore substantive issues in child sexual abuse from survivors' perspective
- to explore survivors' attitudes to a national survey
- to explore methods of approaching the general population

Carried out:

- group discussion between research team and 7 known survivors, net-worked through a Rape Crisis Centre
- depth interviews with 13 known survivors; 9 women and 4 men, networked through counsellors and other professionals working in the field
- depth interviews with 7 members of the general population; 4 women and 3 men recruited by field interviewers according to simple quota

Documents used in Phase Two:

- Letter inviting survivors to participate in study; copies distributed to professionals working with adult survivors through personal contacts and SCOSAC newsletter
- Topic guide for survivor interviews
- Letters of introduction used when recruiting for general population interviews: 2 approaches: (a) and (b)
- Topic guide used for general population interviews

Head Office: 35 NORTHAMPTON SQUARE,   Field and DP Office: 100 KINGS ROAD,
LONDON EC1V 0AX   BRENTWOOD, ESSEX CM14 4LX
Tel: 071-250 1866 Fax: 071-250 1524   Tel: 0277 200600 Fax: 0277 214117

March 1992

LETTER TO SURVIVORS:PHASE 1

Feasibility study for a national survey of child sexual abuse

Can you help us with our research?

The Department of Health is concerned to understand the nature and extent of child sexual abuse in this country, so that appropriate resources and support can be provided. To help plan these services, the Department is considering a large scale national survey of the circumstances and prevalence of child sexual abuse (the proportion of adults who have experienced some form of sexual abuse during their childhood). It is very important that research of this kind is designed with care and sensitivity, and so the Department has commissioned a preliminary study to look at the feasibility of a major survey in this field.

Social and Community Planning Research (SCPR) has been asked to carry out this preliminary work. SCPR is an independent research institute which carries out surveys and in-depth studies on a wide range of social issues, and has experience of researching sensitive subjects, including sexual experiences and attitudes.

As part of our preparation for this study, we would like to meet some adult survivors, in order to sharpen our understanding of sexual abuse, and to get advice and feedback on the design and planning of the study. If you can help us with this research, and think you might be willing to be interviewed, just complete the slip at the bottom of the page, and return it in the pre-paid envelope. Alternatively, you can phone Liz Spencer or Deborah Ghate at SCPR (071 250 1866) for more details about the project. The interviews would be very informal and completely confidential.

We do hope you feel able to take part, as we are sure that your experience and perspective would be extremely valuable for the study as a whole.

Liz Spencer
Deborah Ghate

Feasibility study for a national survey of child sexual abuse

I am interested in taking part in this study, and would like to know more about it

NAME (please print):

ADDRESS:

DAYTIME TELEPHONE NUMBER:

P5214. PHASE 2 DEPTH INTERVIEWS   TOPIC GUIDE: SURVIVOR INTERVIEWS

Biographical details

(Record gender and ethnic background - ask later if necessary)

Age

Relationship status

Children   - number
             - ages

Who live with at present

Employment/occupation

Age left school/full-time education
             - any qualifications

Age left home (if appropriate)

Religion
             - do you belong to a particular religion?
             - Religion now and in childhood

Childhood circumstances (I'd like to ask you a bit about your childhood
                         [birth - 16 years])

Family details:
             - number of brothers and sisters and ages
             - own position in family
             - parents
             - other close relatives
             - who else is there in your family?

Who cared for you when you were a child?
             - changes over time
             - one/both parents
             - other relative(s)
             - in care

Who else lived with you at the time

Who else lived with you at the time

Did you move house/area
             - how many times?
             - did you always live in the same house?
             - how many different places did you live in when you were a
               child?
             - how many people lived in the same house?
             - how many people shared your room/on your own?
             - age at each move (if can remember)
             - type of area (in country or in town)

How many schools attended
             - type (day or boarding/co-ed or single sex)
             - age at transfer

Employment/occupation of parents (other adults)
- (both FT/PT)
- how busy were parents?
- childcare arrangements

Family finances
- remember being comfortable/hard up

Childhood relationships and family atmosphere

Within the family

(General questions about childhood ??happy ??got on together - eg: thinking back to your childhood, would you say that you were generally happy as a child, or not?)

How do you feel your parents (adults) got on with each other
- shared interests/spent much time together
- talked to each other
- any arguments/rows/fights
- was there any physical violence

How did the children get on with parents (ask for each parent/carer separately)
- as a family did you do things together/spend much time together?
- were parents (adults) strict? liberal (easy going)?
- how much freedom/independence did you have?
- how much responsibility did you/eldest child have?
- were you ever punished/how/any physical punishment?
- did you feel able to talk to your parents (about feelings etc and if worried/frightened about anything)?
- any differences between own and sibling relationships with parents?

How did children get on with each other
- how got on with brothers and sisters
- played together much
- could you talk to each other

Outside the family

[Did your family have much contact with friends/neighbours/other relatives
- how much/how often
- what? eg visiting or being visited
- how felt about it/enjoyed?]
- (open or closed family) was yours a fairly outgoing family, or did you keep yourselves to yourselves?

Own friendships
- any special friends - from school or locally
- visiting each other's homes etc
- how got on with teachers
- any friendships with other adults/relatives - anybody else you were close to when you were a child?
- did you talk about your feelings etc to friends if worried or frightened?

General perception of family 'atmosphere'

How affectionate/demonstrative/tactile were the family

(Sex education and first knowledge)

In general, how private were your family over such things as
- getting undressed
- going to the bathroom
- taking baths (any bathing together)
- covering up rather than seeing each other naked

Did your parents (adults) talk to you about growing up and (sexual development/how bodies develop)?
- periods, breasts, pubic hair, etc
- modesty in clothing, ways of sitting etc

Did they talk with you about sex and sexual relationships
- tell/explain/answer questions
- ever tell you anything about things like masturbation, for example?

How comfortable was your family with the subject of sex
- eg reactions to sex scenes on TV etc
- reactions to newspaper stories etc

If at boarding school
- how much privacy was there
- any information about sex and sexual relationships

Peer group discussions; playground talk, friends experiences of sex, did you feel that you were at same level/development as others - did what they say ring true?

How found out about facts of life/sex education

How first became aware of sex (generally)
- from whom/where/stages/process

Can you remember what impressions you formed of what sex might be like?

Before you were 16 did you ever see any porn/blue material

(Childhood sexual experiences)

Did you have <u>any</u> kind of experience that you would now consider sexual before you were 16? (Sexual in retrospect)

When did you first have what you would <u>now</u> consider a sexual experience of any kind (probe for additional experiences apart from sexual intercourse eg fondling, exhibitionism, kissing etc). For example: kissing, petting, any kind of touching

(Probe for earlier sexual experiences ie pre 16, pre 12/13. Try to establish chronological order, and how they pinpoint timing)

For each encounter (or series of encounters if happened more than once with same person)

- own age (at the outset of each) how old were you when it first happened?

- who with (peer, relative, known adult, stranger etc)
  (if known, how close was relationship)

- age, gender and ethnicity of partner

- number, ages and gender of anyone else involved

- can you tell me a bit about/describe for me what happened/tended to happen (sexually)

- what sort of things were done to you/did you have to do to other people

- what was done to you/you had to do

- (get general picture if over many years etc)

- who initiated first encounter (how did it start)

- where did it happen/tend to happen

- if you had to describe it at the time, did you want it to happen or not?

- how did it come about/how did the other person get you
  involved/what strategies were used (eg mutual desire, promises, bribes, favours, entrapment, threats, force etc)

- how much did you know what would happen/understand what was happening (link back to extent of sexual knowledge)

- did you think it was normal or OK/or there was anything 'wrong'/'immoral' (at the time or later)?

- feelings at the time (eg pleasure, happiness, fear - or what - pain, anger, betrayal etc) about the event about the person

- how much secrecy was involved/were you asked to keep it
  secret/how asked (use of threats?) Do you think anyone else knew what was going on?

- did it happen more than once with same person(s)/how many times/over what period of time

- any changes in over time in
  - type of sexual contact/activity/things that happened sexually
  - circumstances - how or where it happened
  - ways of gaining their compliance
  - number of people involved
  - feelings about events/person
  - secrecy/keeping it secret

When/how/why did it stop then
- was it because of something they did (eg different tactic or refusal or feeling older and more powerful) or because of other people or circumstances

- how felt when it stopped

know or suspect partner/abuser was having sexual ? with anyone else

- number, age and other details

Other ways of CSA being discovered

If did not tell directly as a child

        - why not
        - did they try to give other signs / behave differently
        - did they think anyone else knew or suspected what was going on

Effects - short and long term

What were the after-effects, both short and long term (if more than one experience/story of CSA, try to attribute effects accordingly - if appropriate - or establish different effects/responses and WHY affected them differently)

How affected relationships with
        - partner / perpetrator
        - family
        - peers etc
        - at the time / subsequently

How affected educational achievement

How affected mental/emotional/physical health (self esteem, depression anxiety etc)

How long did these effects last

How feel now

Any effects on
        - adult relationships
        - adult sexual relationships

Any effects on choice of partner (if applicable)

Sexual histories/lifestyle since adulthood

Current situation
        - are they in a sexual relationship, or more than one.

        - age and gender of partner(s)

        - describe own sexual orientation

Previous situation
        - any sexual relationships/partners prior to current one(s) and since adulthood (since 16 yrs ?)

        - age and gender of partners

Were all these wanted/consensual, or any adult experiences of unwanted/forced sex?

(If unwanted/forced

- how many? - events/perpetrators

- who, and nature of relationship

- circumstances

- type of sexual activity

- feelings and effects

- disclosed?, any action taken, outcome?

Any sexual experiences/contact with someone younger than self?

- how much younger

Experience of paid sex (as client or ....?!)

- age and gender of partner(s)

- number of occasions

Ever looked at "blue" videos or literature (pornography of any kind)

General health

Perception of own general health - physical/emotional/mental

Overview of effects of CSA (if appropriate)

Own experience or counselling or therapy

Advice to survivors

Experience of taking part in the study

How felt about (for self and other respondents)

- in general
- language
- embarrasment
- memory / recall
- accuracy / comprehensiveness / honesty
- interviewer manner

How felt about subject matter covered

How would you feel if we were to have asked about:

- own sexual experiences with people under 16 / under 13

    - who/ number involved/ nature of relationship/ gender

    - circumstances

    - who initiated

    - how did it come about, was it consensual/coerced

    - types of sexual activity

    - gender of partners (victims)

    - any other adults/perpetrators/age and gender

    - ever disclosed by self or partner

    - any action taken/ outcome

    - own feelings at the time

    - own feelings now

- own use of force / violence in sexual encounters

Head Office: 35 NORTHAMPTON SQUARE,
LONDON EC1V 0AX
Tel: 071-250 1866 Fax: 071-250 1524

SCPR

Field and DP Office: 100 KINGS ROAD,
BRENTWOOD, ESSEX CM14 4LX
Tel: 0277 200600 Fax: 0277 214117

APPROACH (a)   May 1992

Feasibility study for a national survey of childhood and children's understanding of sex

This study of childhood and children's understanding of sex is being carried out by Social and Community Planning Research for the Department of Health. Information of this kind is very important for targeting resources and planning services for children and young people, in such areas as: health and development, sex education, and personal safety for children who may be at risk of unwanted sexual experiences. The survey is being carried out among adults rather than amongst children and young people to enable us to explore changes over time.

As there is very little reliable information on this subject for Britain as a whole, and because it is important that research of this kind is designed with care and sensitivity, the Department of Health has commissioned this preliminary study to look at whether or not a study of this kind is possible.

Social and Community Planning Research (SCPR) is an independent research institute which carries out surveys and in-depth studies on a wide range of social issues, and has substantial experience of researching sensitive subjects. In preparation for this particular study, and to help us in the design of the survey, we would like to talk to a cross section of adults in the general population.

We do hope that you are able to take part as we are sure that your experience and perspective would be extremely valuable for the study as a whole. If you would like further information about this research, you can contact Liz Spencer or Deborah Ghate at SCPR (071 250 1866). The interviews will be very informal and completely confidential.

Liz Spencer   Deborah Ghate

Thank you for agreeing to take part in this study. We look forward to seeing you on:

Date:...

Time:...

Place:..

Head Office: 35 NORTHAMPTON SQUARE, SCPR *Field and DP Office: 100 KINGS ROAD,*
LONDON EC1V 0AX *BRENTWOOD, ESSEX CM14 4LX*
Tel: 071-250 1866 Fax: 071-250 1524 *Tel: 0277 200600 Fax: 0277 214117*

APPROACH (b) May 1992

Feasibility study for a national survey of childhood and family life

This study of childhood and aspects of family life is being carried out by Social and Community Planning Research for the Department of Health. Information on changing patterns of family life, child rearing, and childhood experiences is important for targeting resources and planning the services that may be needed by children and young people. The survey is being carried out among adults rather than amongst children to enable us to explore changes over time.

As there is very little reliable information on this subject for Britain as a whole, and because it is important that research of this kind is designed with care and sensitivity, the Department of Health has commissioned this preliminary study to look at whether or not a study of this kind is possible.

Social and Community Planning Research (SCPR) is an independent research institute which carries out surveys and in-depth studies on a wide range of social issues, and has substantial experience of researching personal or sensitive subjects. In preparation for this particular study, and to help us in the design of the survey, we would like to talk to a cross section of adults in the general population.

We do hope that you are able to take part as we are sure that your experience and perspective would be extremely valuable for the study as a whole. If you would like further information about this research, you can contact Liz Spencer or Deborah Ghate at SCPR (071 250 1866). The interviews will be very informal and completely confidential.

Liz Spencer Deborah Ghate

Liz Spencer *Deborah Ghate*

Thank you for agreeing to take part in this study. We look forward to seeing you on:

Date:...

Time:...

Place:...

<u>P5214. PHASE 2 DEPTH INTERVIEWS   TOPIC GUIDE: GENERAL POPULATION INTERVIEWS</u>

<u>Biographical details</u>

(Record gender and ethnic background - ask later if necessary)

Age

Relationship status

Children
         - number
         - ages

Who live with at present

Employment/occupation

Age left school/full-time education
         - any qualifications

Age left home (if appropriate)

[RELIGION]

<u>Childhood circumstances</u>

Family details:
         - number of brothers and sisters and ages
         - own position in family
         - parents
         - other close relatives

Who cared for you when you were a child
         - one/both parents
         - other relative(s)
         - in care

Who else lived with you at the time

Did you move house/area
         - how many times
         - what sort of house/flat
         - how many people lived in the same house
         - how many people shared your room/on your own
         - age at each move (if can remember)

How many schools attended
         - age at transfer

Employment/occupation of parents (other adults) [PROBE FOR FULL TIME OR PART
TIME / CHILDCARE ARRANGEMENTS WHEN PARENTS OUT / HOW BUSY WERE PARENTS]

Family finances
         - remember being comfortable/hard up

Childhood relationships and family atmosphere
==

Within the family

(General question about childhood ???? happy ???? got on together)

How do you feel your parents (adults) got on with each other
- shared interests/spent much time together
- talked to each other
- any arguments/rows/fights
- was there ever any physical violence

How did the children get on with parents (adults)
- as a family did you do things together/spend much time together
- were parents (adults) strict? liberal?
- how much freedom/independence did you have [RESPONSIBILITY]
- were you ever punished/how/any physical punishment
- did you feel able to talk to your parents [ABOUT FEELINGS, WORRIES, INCIDENTS i.e. COMMUNICATION]
- any differences between own and siblings relationships with parents

How did children get on with each other
- how got on with brothers and sisters
- played together much
- could you talk to each other

Outside the family

Did your family have much contact with friends/neighbours/other relatives
- (open or closed family)

Own friendships
- any special friends - from school or local
- visiting each others homes etc
- did you talk about feelings WORRIES INCIDENTS ETC to friends
- [PROBE FOR SPECIAL FRIENDS / CONFIDANTES]
- [EXTENT OF ISOLATION / LONELINESS AS A CHILD]

General perception of family "atmosphere"

Sex education and first knowledge [GIVE INTRO ABOUT RESEARCH BEING INTERESTED IN THE PROCESS OF GROWING UP AND SEXUAL DEVELOPMENT]

How private were your family over such things as
- getting undressed
- going to the bathroom
- taking baths (any bathing together)
- covering up rather than seeing each other naked

Did your parents (adults) talk to you about growing up and sexual development
- periods, breasts, pubic hair, etc
- modestly in clothing, ways of sitting etc
- [MORE DETAIL ON THIS eg PHRASES USED/EXACTLY WHAT TOLD]

Did they talk with you about sex and sexual relationships

                    - tell/explain/answer questions
                    - what told about or reactions to masturbation (??????????)

How comfortable was your family with the subject of sex
                    - e.g. reactions to sexy scenes on TV etc
                    - reactions to newspaper stories etc

[DISCUSSIONS WITH FRIENDS / PLAYGROUND TALK / FRIENDS EXPERIENCES /WHETHER
FELT AT SAME STAGE OF DEVELOPMENT OR DISCOVERY AS FRIENDS]

How did you actually find out
                    - when/where/in stages

[FROM WHAT YOU HAD BEEN TOLD / KNEW, CAN YOU REMEMBER WHAT IMPRESSIONS YOU
FORMED OF WHAT SEX WOULD BE LIKE eg exciting, baffling, dirty ????]

Childhood sexual experiences [GIVE INTRO ABOUT INTEREST IN EARLY EXPERIENCES]

DID YOU HAVE ANY EXPERIENCES - OF ANY KIND - WHICH YOU NOW CONSIDER SEXUAL
BEFORE YOU WERE 16

[PROBE A LOT ON THIS. YOU MAY NEED TO GIVE EXAMPLES LIKE ... PLAYING DOCTORS
AND NURSES, SHOWING PRIVATE PARTS, (SOMEONE EXPOSING THEMSELVES, SOMEONE
MAKING SUGGESTIONS,) FONDLING, KISSING ETC]

[IF THEY HAVE NOTHING TO TELL, TRY THE FOLLOWING:

(●)   ANY UNWANTED EXPERIENCES OF ANY KIND BEFORE 16
(●)   ANY UNWANTED/REGRETTED EXPERIENCES AFTER 16 + CIRCUMSTANCES ETC

THEN OMIT SECTIONS ON DETAILS OF CSA, NARROW ESCAPES, DISCLOSURE, EFFECTS,
SEXUAL HISTORIES AND GENERAL HEALTH - AND MOVE TO LAST 2 SECTIONS:

                    - PREPARATION FOR ADULT LIFE
                    - EXPERIENCE OF TAKING PART IN THE STUDY]

(IF THEY HAVE SOMETHING TO TELL, EXPLAIN THAT YOU WOULD LIKE TO ASK THEM A BIT
ABOUT IT BECAUSE THE STUDY IS INTERESTED IN PERSONAL SAFETY FOR CHILDREN THEN
CONTINUE WITH THE GUIDE AS IT WAS FOR SURVIVORS]

FOR THOSE WITH SOMETHING TO TELL ONLY

For each encounter (or series of encounters if happened more than once with
same person)
                    - own age (at the outset)
                    - who with (per, relative, known adult, stranger etc)
                      (if known, how close was relationship)
                    - age, gender and ethnicity of partner
                    - number, ages and gender of anyone else involved

- what happened - type of activity
                    - circumstances and location
- who initiated first encounter

- wanted or unwanted

- how did it come about/what strategies were used (eg mutual desire, promises, bribes, favours, entrapment, threats, force etc)

- how much did you know what would happen/understand what was happening

- did you think it was OK/or there was anything "wrong£/"immoral"

- feelings at the time (eg pleasure, happiness, fear-of what-, pain, anger, betrayal etc) about the event, about the person (extent of victimisation, if any)

- how much secrecy was involved/were you asked to keep it secret/how asked (use of threats?)

- did it happen more than once with same person(s)/how many times/over what period of time

- any changes over time in - type of sexual contact/activity
                             - ways of gaining their compliance
                             - number of people involved
                             - feelings about events/person
                             - secrecy/keeping it secret

When/how/why did it stop
        - was it because of something they did (eg different tactic or refusal or feeling older and more powerful) or because of other people or circumstances

        - how felt when it stopped

Know or suspect partner/abuser was having sexual ? with anyone else
        - number, age and other details

Attempts and narrow escapes

Any other times when someone attempted to have some kind of sexual contact with you but did not succeed

        - what happened

<u>Disclosures</u>

Ever told anyone

> - who
> - what/how told
> - how many times
> - response of person(s) told / believed or not / supported or not
> - what happened / any formal intervention or reporting and outcome
> - effects of disclosure or outcome on respondent and others
> - feelings about what happened

Other ways of CSA being discovered

If not directly told
> - why not'
> - did they try to give other signs /behave differently
> - did they think anyone else knew or suspected what was going on

<u>Effects - short and long term</u>

What were the after-effects, both short and long term (if more than one experience/story of CSA, try to attribute effects accordingly - if appropriate - or establish different effects/responses and WHY affected them differently)

How affected relationship with
> - partner / perpetrator
> - family
> - peers etc

How affected educational achievement

How affected mental/emotional/physical health (self esteem, depression anxiety etc)

How long did these effects last

How feel now

Any effects on
> - adult relationships
> - adult sexual relationships

Any effects on choice of partner (if applicable)

<u>Sexual histories/lifestyle since adulthood</u>

Current situation
> - are they in a sexual relationship, or more than one
> - age and gender of partner(s)

- own sexual orientation

Previous situation
- any sexual relationships/partners prior to current one(s) and since adulthood (since 16 yrs ?)

- age and gender of partners

Were all these wanted/consensual, or any adult experiences or unwanted/forced sex?

(If unwanted/forced

- how many?   - events/perpetrators
- who, and nature of relationship
- circumstances
- type of sexual activity
- feelings and effects
- disclosed?, any action taken, outcome?

Any sexual experiences/contact with someone younger than self?

- how much younger

Experience of paid sex (as client or ......?!)

- age and gender of partner(s)
- number of occasions

Ever looked at "blue" vidoes or literature (pornography of any kind)

General health

Perception of own general health - physical/emotional/mental

Overview of effects of CSA (if appropriate)

Own experience of counselling or therapy

Advice to survivors

Preparation for adult life

How well prepared do you feel you were for adult relationships/ sexual
relationships by what you were told/found out/happened to you as a child [TAKE
CARE HERE IF THEY DID HAVE UNWANTED SEXUAL EXPERIENCES AS A CHILD]

How much childhood experiences affect adult relationships

What should we tell children / how should we prepare them

Could we do it better
            how?   who?

What should we tell children about personal safety

            how?   who?

Experience of taking part in the study

How felt about (for self and other respondents)

            - in general
            - language
            - embarrassment
            - memory/recall
            - accuracy/comprehensiveness/honesty
            - interviewer manner /type of interviewer
            - subject matter
            - WAS IT WHAT YOU EXPECTED FROM WHAT YOU WERE TOLD

[OMIT THIS SECTION FOR PEOPLE WHO HAVE NOT HAD UNWANTED SEXUAL EXPERIENCES AS
CHILD]

How would you have felt if we were to have asked about:

            - own sexual experiences with people under 16 / 13
            - who/number involved/nature of relationship/gender
            - circumstances
            - who initiated
            - how did it come about, was it consensual /coerced
            - types of sexual activity
            - gender of partners (victims)
            - any other adults/perpetrators/age and gender
            - ever disclosed by self or partner
            - any action taken/outcome
            - own feelings at the time
            - own feelings now
            - own use of force or violence in sexual encounters

Phase Three : 79 semi-structured and structured pre-pilot interviews

During Phase Three the insights gained from the depth interviews were used to help design a research questionnaire which was modified over the course of the three pre-pilots which were carried out between June and September 1992. Because of the sensitivity of the material and the difficulty of producing a structured instrument which would do justice to the complexity of the subject, it was decided to move in stages from a semi-structured to a fully-structured questionnaire, using a modular approach in which new modules could be phased in and old ones retained or phased out as necessary. Eight of the most experienced female SCPR field interviewers were selected to work on the study, all of whom had worked on a previous national survey of sexual attitudes and lifestyles conducted by SCPR. Field interviewers were introduced into the study in stages; this meant that members of the research team continued to conduct interviews themselves throughout the study, and were thus able to assess how the questionnaire was performing in the field at first hand, as well as providing an opportunity to observe the 'performance curve' of field interviewers as more experienced interviewers worked alongside those who were new to the study. Since one of the prime methodological goals of the research was to investigate the most appropriate context in which to present the research to respondents, the three pre-pilots also gave us the opportunity to try out a variety of different approaches.

Pre-pilot one

Four field interviewers worked on the first pre-pilot, alongside the research team. 21 respondents were recruited from four areas (Bradford, Birmingham, Portsmouth and Newcastle) according to a simple quota based on age, sex, marital status and childhood occupational class (that is, parent's occupation).

Pre-pilot two

A further four interviewers joined the team for this pre-pilot, working in Essex, Plymouth, London and Reading. Again, respondents were recruited using a simple quota, and 20 productive interviews were achieved.

Although the general population samples included some adults who had had abusive experiences in childhood, the research team also set up interviews with known survivors for four of the eight interviewers during this stage, to enable field interviewers to gain experience in carrying out structured interviews with respondents of this kind. Three of the survivors had already taken part in depth interviews, and the team were able to compare the results of the structured survey interview with qualitative data, to obtain a picture of how well the emergent structured questionnaire was able to capture the complexity and fine detail of child sexual abuse.

Pre-pilot three

In pre-pilot 3 we moved from quota sampling to a sample of randomly pre-selected addresses obtained from the Postcodes Address File (PAF) in six areas in which interviewers were based; Reading, Essex, Birmingham, Bradford, North London and Portsmouth. Having made contact at an address, the interviewer then carried out a random selection of an adult member of the household by listing all adults resident in the household systematically, using a random number grid to select one adult for interview. Two different approaches were used, and a total of 38 productive interviews were achieved; 29 with the first approach [approach (a)], and 9 with the second [approach (b)]. (Table 1 gives further details of the approaches used).

A summary of this phase together with the documents used is given below.

Phase Three
Aim:

- to develop an approach and presentation context for the survey
- to develop a structured questionnaire and test out a range of modules

Carried out:

- Pre-pilot 1 – quota sample; 21 interviews
- Pre-pilot 2 – quota sample; 20 interviews
      – networked sample of known survivors; 4 interviews
- Pre-pilot 3 – random (PAF) sample; 2 approaches – (a) 29 interviews
                                                                        (b) 9 interviews

Documents used in Phase 3:

- Letter of introduction used in pre-pilot 1 and pre-pilot 2
- Contact sheet for interviews used in pre-pilot 1 and pre-pilot 2
- Letter of introduction, approach (a), used in pre-pilot 3
- Letter of introduction, approach (b), used in pre-pilot 3
- Address Record Form and selection sheet
- Comment slip for respondents [all pre-pilots; supplied with pre-paid envelope]
- Lists of local counselling and support services given to respondents in all pre-pilots
- Postal questionnaire mailed to non-respondents; supplied with pre-paid envelope

Head Office: 35 NORTHAMPTON SQUARE, LONDON EC1V 0AX
Tel: 071-250 1866 Fax: 071-250 1524

SCPR
SOCIAL & COMMUNITY PLANNING RESEARCH

Field and DP Office: 100 KINGS ROAD, BRENTWOOD, ESSEX CM14 4LX
Tel: 0277 200600 Fax: 0277 214117

LETTER TO RESPONDENTS; PRE-PILOTS 1 AND 2

June 1992

Feasibility study for a national survey of childhood and children's understanding of sex

This study of childhood and children's understanding of sex is being carried out by Social and Community Planning Research for the Department of Health. Information of this kind is very important for targeting resources and planning services for children and young people, in such areas as: health and development, sex education, and personal safety for children who may be at risk of unwanted sexual experiences. The survey is being carried out among adults, and explores people's recollections of their own experiences during childhood.

As there is very little reliable information on this subject for Britain as a whole, and because it is important that research of this kind is designed with care and sensitivity, the Department of Health has commissioned this preliminary study to look at whether or not a study of this kind is possible.

Social and Community Planning Research (SCPR) is an independent research institute which carries out surveys and in-depth studies on a wide range of social issues, and has substantial experience of researching sensitive subjects. In preparation for this particular study, and to help us in the design of the national survey, we would like to interview a cross section of adults in the general population.

We do hope that you are able to take part as we are sure that your experience and perspective would be extremely valuable for the study as a whole. It does not matter if there are parts of your childhood which you cannot remember very well, we would still like to be able to include you in the research. The interviews at this stage are quite exploratory, and completely confidential. If you would like further information about the study you can contact Liz Spencer, Bob Erens, or Deborah Ghate at SCPR (071 250 1866).

Liz Spencer   Bob Erens   Deborah Ghate

Survey of Childhood Experiences

P1217/P2   CONTACT SHEET

Q.1 Any contact at address: WRITE IN ADDRESS		

Q.5 Person's estimated age:

	18-59	1 → Q6
	under 18 or 60+	2 → END
	DK	3 → Q6

Q.2 Willing and able to take part?	Yes	1	→	Q3	
	No	2	→	Q5	

Q.6 Code person's sex:

Male	1	→ Q7
Female	2	→ Q7

Q.7 Reason for not taking part **WRITE IN**

Q.3 COMPLETE SCREENING QUESTIONNAIRE

Person is:	In quota	1	→	Q4
	Not in quota	2	→	END

IF NO REASON GIVEN, CODE:

Do you think it had to do with the survey topic?	Yes	1
	No	2
	DK	3

Q.4 WRITE IN SERIAL NUMBER ☐☐☐ → INTERVIEW

Q.1 Any contact at address: WRITE IN ADDRESS		

Q.5 Person's estimated age:

	18-59	1 → Q6
	under 18 or 60+	2 → END
	DK	3 → Q6

Q.2 Willing and able to take part?	Yes	1	→	Q3	
	No	2	→	Q5	

Q.6 Code person's sex:

Male	1	→ Q7
Female	2	→ Q7

Q.7 Reason for not taking part **WRITE IN**

Q.3 COMPLETE SCREENING QUESTIONNAIRE

Person is:	In quota	1	→	Q4
	Not in quota	2	→	END

IF NO REASON GIVEN, CODE:

Do you think it had to do with the survey topic?	Yes	1
	No	2
	DK	3

Q.4 WRITE IN SERIAL NUMBER ☐☐☐ → INTERVIEW

Q.1 Any contact at address: WRITE IN ADDRESS		

Q.5 Person's estimated age:

	18-59	1 → Q6
	under 18 or 60+	2 → END
	DK	3 → Q6

Q.2 Willing and able to take part?	Yes	1	→	Q3	
	No	2	→	Q5	

Q.6 Code person's sex:

Male	1	→ Q7
Female	2	→ Q7

Q.7 Reason for not taking part **WRITE IN**

Q.3 COMPLETE SCREENING QUESTIONNAIRE

Person is:	In quota	1	→	Q4
	Not in quota	2	→	END

IF NO REASON GIVEN, CODE:

Do you think it had to do with the survey topic?	Yes	1
	No	2
	DK	3

Q.4 WRITE IN SERIAL NUMBER ☐☐☐ → INTERVIEW

Head Office: 35 NORTHAMPTON SQUARE, LONDON EC1V 0AX Tel: 071-250 1866 Fax: 071-250 1524

Field and DP Office: 100 KINGS ROAD, BRENTWOOD, ESSEX CM14 4LX Tel: 0277 200600 Fax: 0277 214117

APPROACH (a)   September 1992

Feasibility study for a national survey of childhood and children's understanding and knowledge of sex

Please help us with our research

This study of childhood and children's understanding and knowledge of sex is being carried out by Social and Community Planning Research for the Department of Health. Information of this kind is very important for targeting resources and planning services for children and young people, in such areas as: health and development, sex education, and personal safety for children who may be at risk of unwanted sexual experiences. The survey is being carried out among adults rather than amongst children and young people to enable us to explore changes over time.

As there is very little reliable information on this subject for Britain as a whole, and because it is important that research of this kind is designed with care and sensitivity, the Department of Health has commissioned this preliminary study to look at whether or not a study of this kind is possible.

Social and Community Planning Research (SCPR) is an independent research institute which carries out surveys and in-depth studies on a wide range of social issues, and has substantial experience of researching sensitive subjects. In preparation for this particular study, and to help us in the design of the survey, we would like to talk to a cross section of adults in the general population.

Your address was chosen at random from the list of addresses in your area to which the Post Office deliver mail. An interviewer from SCPR will contact you in the next few weeks to explain how we would like an adult member of your household to help us with this important new study. We do hope that you are able to take part as we are sure that your experience and perspective would be extremely valuable for the study as a whole. It does not matter if there are parts of your childhood which you cannot remember well, we would still like to be able to include you in the research. If you would like further information about this research, you can contact the researchers, Liz Spencer, Deborah Ghate or Bob Erens at SCPR (071 250 1866). The interviews will be very informal and completely confidential: **no information will be passed on in a way which would identify you.**

Yours sincerely

Liz Spencer   Bob Erens   Deborah Ghate

Head Office: 35 NORTHAMPTON SQUARE,   Field and DP Office: 100 KINGS ROAD,
LONDON EC1V 0AX   BRENTWOOD, ESSEX CM14 4LX
Tel: 071-250 1866 Fax:071-250 1524   Tel: 0277 200600 Fax: 0277 214117

APPROACH (b)   September 1992

Feasibility study for a national survey of public attitudes to child sexual abuse

Please help us with our research

This study of public attitudes to child sexual abuse is being carried out by Social and
Community Planning Research for the Department of Health. Information of this kind is very
important for targeting resources and planning services for children and young people, in such
areas as: sex education for children, and personal safety for children who may be at risk of
unwanted sexual experiences.

As there is very little reliable information on this subject for Britain as a whole, and because
it is important that research of this kind is designed with care and sensitivity, the Department
of Health has commissioned this preliminary study to look at whether or not a study of this
kind is possible.

Social and Community Planning Research (SCPR) is an independent research institute which
carries out surveys and in-depth studies on a wide range of social issues, and has substantial
experience of researching sensitive subjects. In preparation for this particular study, and to
help us in the design of the survey, we would like to talk to a cross section of adults in the
general population.

Your address was chosen at random from the list of addresses in your area to which the Post
Office deliver mail. An interviewer from SCPR will contact you in the next few weeks to
explain how we would like an adult member of your household to help us with this important
new study. We do hope that you are able to take part as we are sure that your experience and
perspective would be extremely valuable for the study as a whole. If you would like further
information about this research, you can contact the researchers, Liz Spencer, Deborah Ghate
or Bob Erens at SCPR (071 250 1866). The interviews will be very informal and completely
confidential: **no information will be passed on in a way which would identify you.**

Yours sincerely

Liz Spencer   Bob Erens   Deborah Ghate

Head Office: 35 NORTHAMPTON SQUARE,   Field and DP Office: 100 KINGS ROAD,
LONDON EC1V 0AX   BRENTWOOD, ESSEX CM14 4LX
Tel: 071-250 1866 Fax: 071-250 1524   Tel: 0277 200600 Fax: 0277 214117

P1217/P3   ADDRESS RECORD FORM (ARF)   September 1992

Survey of Public Attitudes
to Child Sexual Abuse

ADDRESS   a) ENTER FULL NAME OF SELECTED PERSON:

Title: Mr/Mrs/Miss/Ms _____

First name(s): _____

Surname: _____

b) ENTER DAYTIME TEL.NO. _____

Interviewer Name ...   ... and No.   11-14

CALLS RECORD (Note <u>all</u> calls, even if no reply)   TNC 15-16

CALL NUMBER	01	02	03	04	05	06	07	08	09	10	11	12
TIME OF DAY:												
Up to noon	1	1	1	1	1	1	1	1	1	1	1	1
1201-1400	2	2	2	2	2	2	2	2	2	2	2	2
1401-1700	3	3	3	3	3	3	3	3	3	3	3	3
1701-1900	4	4	4	4	4	4	4	4	4	4	4	4
1900 or later	5	5	5	5	5	5	5	5	5	5	5	5
DATE:												
i) Day (Mon = 1, Tues = 2 etc)												
ii) Date												
iii) Month												
EXACT TIME OF CALL												

NOTES

ALWAYS RETURN ARF SEPARATELY FROM QUESTIONNAIRE

```
┌─────────────────────────────────────┐                          RING
│  COMPLETE AS FAR AS FINAL OUTCOME   │                          FINAL
└─────────────────────────────────────┘                         OUTCOME
                                                                  CODE
```

1. IS THIS ADDRESS TRACEABLE, RESIDENTIAL AND OCCUPIED?

Yes	A **GO TO Q.3**
No	B **ANSWER Q.2**

IF NO AT Q.1   17-18

2. WHY NOT?

Insufficient address	01	
Not traced (**call office before returning**)	02	
Not yet built/not yet ready for occupation	03	
Derelict/demolished	04	*
		END
Empty	05	
Business/industrial only (no private dwellings)	06	
Institution only (no private dwellings)	07	
_____ Other (**please give details**)	08	

3. CONTACT SUMMARY (RING ONE CODE ONLY)

Information has been obtained about occupants at address	B→ **SEL- ECTION SHEET**

NO INFORMATION OBTAINED ABOUT OCCUPANTS AT ADDRESS, BECAUSE:

- no contact with anyone at address after 4 or more calls	22→ **END**
- complete refusal of information about occupants	23→ **END**

4. OUTCOME OF INTERVIEW ATTEMPTS

CODE ONE

Interview obtained: - Full	51	*
		END
- Partial	52	

No interview obtained:

- No person aged 18-60 in selected D.U.	70	
- No contact with selected person after 4+ calls	71	
- Personal refusal by selected person	72	
- Proxy refusal (on behalf of selected person)	73	
- Broken appointment, no recontact	74	
- Ill at home during survey period	75	*
- Away/in hospital during survey period	76	**END**
- Selected person senile/incapacitated	77	
- Inadequate English	78	
Other reason	79	

```
┌─────────────────────────────────────────────────────────────┐
│  FULL REASON FOR OUTCOME CODES 71-79                         │
│                                                             │
│                                                             │
│                                                             │
│                                                             │
└─────────────────────────────────────────────────────────────┘
```

Head Office: 35 NORTHAMPTON SQUARE,
LONDON EC1V 0AX
Tel: 071-250 1866 Fax: 071-250 1524

SCPR
SOCIAL & COMMUNITY PLANNING RESEARCH

Field and DP Office: 100 KINGS ROAD,
BRENTWOOD, ESSEX CM14 4LX
Tel: 0277 200600 Fax: 0277 214117

P.1217/P3   September 1992

SURVEY OF PUBLIC ATTITUDES TO CHILD SEXUAL ABUSE

<u>Respondent Selection Sheet</u>

SERIAL NO.   [|]   ←   Selection Digit
(write in
from ARF)

Q1a) | At the present time, how many households live
at this address (**READ OUT ADDRESS ON ARF**)? By
household I mean people who use the same living
room or share at least one meal each day.

One	1	ASK b)
2 or more	2	GO TO Q2

b) | May I ask, how many people aged between 18 and
60 years live here as part of this household?

ENTER NUMBER	[	]	→ GO TO Q4
OR CODE: One person household	01	ASK c)
None	00	END

c) | **ENTER FULL NAME OF PERSON ON ARF AND PROCEED
WITH INTRODUCTION TO SURVEY AND INTERVIEW.**

2+ households:
Q2) | **SELECTION REQUIRED:**

a) | RECORD TOTAL NUMBER OF DWELLING UNITS AT THE ADDRESS: [|]

b) | List each D.U. below in grid (LIST SYSTEMATICALLY,
EG. FROM LOWEST TO HIGHEST ROOM NUMBER, BOTTOM TO
TOP ETC.)

'DWELLING UNITS'	'DU' CODE
	1
	2
	3
	4
	5
	6
	7
	8
	9

MAKE D.U. SELECTION
USING GRID OVERLEAF
AND ASK Q3

At Selected D.U.

Q3a) May I ask, how many people aged between 18 and
60 years live her as part of this household?

ENTER NUMBER			→ GO TO Q4
OR CODE: One person household	01		ASK b)
None	00		END

b) ENTER FULL NAME OF PERSON ON ARF AND PROCEED
WITH INTRODUCTION TO SURVEY AND INTERVIEW.

2+ persons:

Q4a) SELECTION REQUIRED. LIST ALL PERSONS 18-60 IN
GRID BELOW IN ALPHABETICAL ORDER BY FIRST NAME.

FIRST NAMES	PERSON CODE	
	1	
	2	
	3	
	4	MAKE PERSON SELECTION
	5	USING GRID, THEN
	6	GO TO c)
	7	
	8	
	9	

b) USE GRID BELOW TO SELECT. GO DOWN COLUMN REPRESENTING TOTAL DU/PERSONS UNTIL
YOU COME TO THE ROW FOR THE <u>SELECTION DIGIT</u> (LAST DIGIT OF SERIAL NUMBER).
THE NUMBER GIVEN WHERE COLUMN AND ROW MEET IS THE <u>DU CODE/PERSON CODE</u> OF D.U. or
PERSON TO INTERVIEW. RING DU CODE AT Q2a)/PERSON CODE AT Q4a).

SELECTION DIGIT (LAST DIGIT OF SERIAL NUMBER)	DU CODE/TOTAL PERSONS IN HOUSEHOLD/(ADDRESS)							
	2	3	4	5	6	7	8	9 or more
0	1	2	3	2	1	5	4	7
1	2	3	1	4	3	6	5	9
2	1	2	2	5	4	3	1	4
3	2	1	4	3	5	7	6	8
4	1	3	2	1	6	2	1	6
5	2	1	3	5	1	7	4	2
6	1	2	4	3	2	5	3	1
7	2	1	3	2	4	1	7	5
8	1	3	2	1	3	4	2	6
9	2	2	1	4	5	6	8	3

c) ENTER FULL NAME OF SELECTED PERSON ON ARF AND PROCEED
WITH INTRODUCTION TO SURVEY AND INTERVIEW

Head Office: 35 NORTHAMPTON SQUARE,
LONDON ECIV 0AX
Tel: 071-250 1866 Fax: 071-250 1524

Field and DP Office: 100 KINGS ROAD,
BRENTWOOD, ESSEX CM14 4LX
Tel: 0277 200600 Fax: 0277 214117

COMMENT SLIP: USED IN ALL PRE-PILOTS

September 1992

Thank you for taking part in this survey.

If you have any comments for the research team, please send them to us on the slip below. A pre-paid envelope is provided.

Alternatively, you are welcome to telephone Liz Spencer, Deborah Ghate or Bob Erens at SCPR on 071-250 1866.

P1217/P3   **September 1992**

Feasibility Study for a National Survey of Childhood and Children's Understanding and Knowledge of Sex.

(Please give your comments below):

SCOSAC

Registered Charity No. 291918

Standing Committee On Sexually Abused Children

COUNSELLING SERVICES IN GREATER LONDON AND THE HOME COUNTIES FOR ADULT WOMEN WHO WERE SEXUALLY ABUSED AS GIRLS

SCOSAC over this year has had hundreds of enquiries from women looking for counselling services to deal with their experience of child sexual abuse.

We are concerned that the services available are too few to meet all womens needs. However, the first problem for the women is finding out about the few services that are there, and it is in response to that need that we have produced the following list.

Before compiling this list we called to ensure that as from December 1991 the following services are in existence, but it is has not been possible for us to determine the type of service available or indeed its quality. We can only suggest that women give these services a try and if things do not work out with one to try others.

73 St Charles Square, London W10 6EJ Tel: 081 960 6376/969 4808 Fax: 081 960 1464

LONDON

WEST LONDON

- **LONDON RAPE CRISIS LINE:**
  PO Box 69, London, WC1X 9NJ
  Tel: 071 837 1600
- **SANCTUARY:**
  PO Box 2615, London W14 0DW
  Tel: 071 371 4666/071 371 4333
- **SOUTHALL BLACK WOMENS CENTRE:**
  86 Northcote Avenue, Southall, Middlesex
  Tel: 081 843 0578
- **WOMEN AND GIRLS NETWORK:**
  BCM 8887, London, WC1N 3XX
  Tel: 071 978 8887
- **MUSLIM WOMENS HELPLINE:**
  Tel: 081 908 6715/081 904 8193

NORTH LONDON

- **ASIAN GIRLS GROUP:**
  8 Manor Gardens, London N7.
  Tel: 071 272 4231
- **CAMDEN LESBIAN INCEST SURVIVORS GROUP:**
  c/o Camden Lesbian Centre and Black Lesbian Group, 54-56 Phoenix Road, London, NW1 1ES.
  Tel: 071 383 5405
- **SPECTRUM INCEST INTERVENTION PROJECT:**
  7, Endymion Road, London, N4 1EE
  Tel: 081 348 0196
- **STEFFIE BROWN GROUP:**
  Hoxton Collective, 1 Arden House, Myrtle Walk, Pitfield Street, London N1 6QD
- **WOMEN AND MEDICAL PRACTICE:**
  40, Turnpike Lane, London, N8 0PS
  Tel: 081 888 2782
- **WOMENS THERAPY CENTRE**
  6, Manor Gardens, London, N7 6LA
  Tel: 071 263 6200

EAST LONDON

- **CHRISTIAN WOMEN SURVIVORS GROUP:**
  c/o St John the Baptist Church, 3 King Edwards Road, London, E8
- **OFF CENTRE:**
  25, Hackney Grove, London, E8
  Tel: 081 986 4016
- **TOWER HAMLETS COUNSELLING SERVICE:**
  1st Floor Oxford House, Derbyshire Street, London, E2
  Tel: 071 739 3082

SOUTH LONDON

- **GREENWICH SEXUAL ABUSE WORKING GROUP:**
  Women's Unit, 45 Hare Street, Woolwich, London, SE18
  Tel: 081 854 8888 Ext. 5818/5815
- **GYPSY HILL GROUP:**
  Community Flat, 11a Camden Hill Road, London, SE19 1NX
  Tel: 081 766 6034/071 326 0333
- **MAYA PROJECT:**
  45 New Kings Road, London, SW6 4SD
  Tel: 071 736 4016
- **SHANTI:**
  1A, Dalbury House, Edmondsbury Court, Ferndale Road, London, SW9 8AP
  Tel: 071 733 8581
- **SOUTH LAMBETH SELF HELP GROUP:**
  Lambeth women and childrens health project, 407 Wandsworth Road, London, SW8
  Tel: 071 737 7151
- **TEENAGE IMFORMATION NETWORK (TIN):**
  102, Harper Road, London, SE1 6AQ
  Tel: 071 403 2444
- **WOMENS ADVICE AND COUNSELLING SERVICE:**
  The Albany, Douglas Way, Deptford, London, SE8
  Tel: 081 692 6268

BEDFORDSHIRE

- BEDFORDSHIRE INCEST SURVIVORS:
  The Moorings, Vandyke Road, Leighton
  Buzzord, Beds.
  Tel: 0525 851 221
- BEDFORDSHIRE SEXUAL ABUSE
  HELPLINE:
  12 Oxford Road, Luton, Beds LU1 3AX
  Tel: 0582 33592

ESSEX

- CENTRE AGAINST SEXUAL ASSAULT ON
  CHILDREN:
  96 Bishopsfield, Harlow, CM18 6UW
  Tel: 0279 444487
- CHELMSFORD RAPE CRISIS:
  PO Box 566, Chelmsford, Essex CM2 8YP
  Tel: 0245 492123
- COLCHESTER RAPE CRISIS:
  PO Box 548, Colchester, Essex
  Tel: 0206 769795
- SOUTHEND RAPE AND INCEST CRISIS
  LINE:
  58 Queens Road, Southend on Sea SS1
  1PZ
  Tel: 0702 347933
- SOUTH ESSEX RAPE AND INCEST
  CRISIS CENTRE:
  Bridge House, 160 Bridge Road, Grays
  Thurrock, Essex RM 17 6DB
  Tel: 0375 380609

HERTFORDSHIRE

- HERTS AREA RAPE CRISIS:
  PO Box 21, Ware, Herts SG12 1AA
  Tel: 07072 76512
- SOUTH WEST HERTS RAPE CRISIS:
  C/O Council of Voluntary Services, St
  Thomas Centre, Langley Road, Watford,
  Herts.
  Tel: 0923 241600
- HERTS INCEST SURVIVORS GROUP:
  Tel: 0442 235890

KENT

- MEDWAY RAPE CRISIS:
  The Whitehouse. Chatham, Kent.
  Tel: 0634 710059/0634 811703
- SANCTUARY:
  PO Box 23, Gillingham, Kent. ME7 1AA.
  Tel: 0634 378300/0622 691430

SURREY

- FARNHAM FAMILY CENTRE:
  East Street, Farnham.
  Tel: 0252 733855
- KINGSTON WOMENS CENTRE:
  169 Canbory Park Gardens, Kingston-
  upon-Thames.
  Tel: 081 541 1964
- CROYDON RAPE AND SEXUAL ABUSE
  SUPPORT CENTRE:
  PO Box 908, London SE25 5EL
  Tel: 081 684 2186
- SUTTON WOMENS CENTRE:
  3 Palmerston Road, Sutton, Surrey SM1
  4QL.
  Tel: 081 661 1991

SUSSEX

- BRIGHTON RAPE CRISIS LINE:
  PO Box 323, Brighton, BN2 2TY.
  Tel: 0273 203773
- SURVIVORS NETWORK:
  PO Box 188, Brighton BN1 7JW.
  Tel: 0273 566555
- CRAWLEY RAPE CRISIS:
  PO Box 170, Crawley West Sussex, RH11
  6YD.
  Tel: 0293 511595
- BRIGHTON WOMEN'S THERAPY AND
  COUNSELLING SERVICE:
  2nd Floor, 79 Buckingham Road, Brighton,
  BN1 3RJ
  Tel: 0273 749800

OTHER USEFUL ORGANISATIONS (FEE PAYING)

● **BRITISH ASSOCIATION OF PSYCHOTHERAPY:**
37, Mapesbury Road, London, NW2 4HJ
Tel: 081 452 9823
Will refer to a therapist

● **BRITISH ASSOCIATION FOR COUNSELLING:**
1, Regent Place, Rugby, CV21 2PJ
Write with a stamped addressed envelope and they will send a list of counsellors

● **GESTALT THERAPY CENTRE:**
64, Warwick Road, St Albans, Herts. AL1 4DL
Tel: 0727 864806

P1217

SUPPORT SERVICES
BRADFORD, LEEDS, MANCHESTER

BRADFORD RAPE CRISIS
* 0274 308270

LEEDS RAPE CRISIS
* 0532 441323

TOUCHLINE -LEEDS
(Face to face and telephone counselling for adult and child survivors
of child sexual abuse, and mothers of sexually abused children)
* 0532 457777

YORK RAPE CRISIS
* 0904 610917

MANCHESTER RAPE CRISIS
* 061 228 3602

MERIDIAN -MANCHESTER
(Counselling and support for women and men survivors of child
sexual abuse)
* 061 232 9896

SUBAH -MANCHESTER
(Support for Asian women and girls who have beeen sexually abused)
* 061 274 3836

```
┌─────────────────────────────────────────────────────────────┐
│                                                             │
│                  SCOSAC                                     │
│              TRAINING AND CONSULTANCY LTD                   │
│  73 St Charles Square London W10 6EJ  Tel: 081 960 6376/969 4808  Fax: 081 960 1464  │
└─────────────────────────────────────────────────────────────┘
```

SUPPORT SERVICES

PORTSMOUTH RAPE CRISIS
- P.O. Box 3, South Sea, Hampshire.
- Tel: 0705 669511

PLYMOUTH RAPE CRISIS
- c/o Box A, Virginia House, Palace Street, Plymouth PL OFQ
- Tel: 0752 223584

READING RAPE CRISIS
- P.O. Box 9, 17 Chatham Street, Reading, Berkshire RG1 7JF
- Tel: 0734 575577

HEREFORD RAPE CRISIS
- Tel: 0432 341494

SHROPSHIRE RAPE CRISIS
- P.O. Box 89, Wellington, Telford TF1 1TZ
- Tel: 0952 504666

TYNESIDE RAPE CRISIS CENTRE
- 34 Grainger Street, Newcastle-upon-Tyne N1
- Tel: 091 232 9858

BIRMINGHAM RAPE CRISIS
- P.O. Box 558, Birmingham
- Tel: 021 233 2122 & 021 233 2655

SURVIVORS
- c/o Walsall Relate, Walsall, West Midlands

ONE IN FOUR
- Box 8, c/o Coventry Voluntary Services Council, 28 Corporation Street, Coventry CV1 1AB
- Tel: 0203 676606

OTHER USEFUL SERVICES

- Brook Advisory Centre, 233 Tottenham Court Road, London W1. Tel: 071 323 1522
- Legal Helpline (Birmingham) Tel: 021 454 7996 & 021 233 4700
- NSPCC Helpline (adults) Tel: 0800 800 500

SCOSAC also holds lists of services for Mothers/Carers of children who have been sexually abused, Male survivors and Partners of people who have been sexually abused.

Head Office: 35 NORTHAMPTON SQUARE,
LONDON EC1V 0AX
Tel: 071-250 1866 Fax: 071-250 1524

Field and DP Office: 100 KINGS ROAD,
BRENTWOOD, ESSEX CM14 4LX
Tel: 0277 200600 Fax: 0277 214117

September 17th 1992

Dear

Feasibility study for a national survey of childhood and children's understanding and knowledge of sex

A short while ago, one of our interviewers called at your home to ask you if you would be willing to take part in the above survey, which we are carrying out for the Department of Health.

We understand from the interviewer who called on you that you were not willing to be interviewed, however, may we ask you to spare us a few minutes of your time to answer the question below?

In all our surveys we are entirely dependent on the co-operation of the public, and it is particularly important for us to know why some people decline to be interviewed. If we do not have these details, we cannot tell whether the information we <u>do</u> have is representative of the whole population. The results of studies such as this one are used to help plan important services for members of the public, and so it is vital that our results are as accurate as possible.

All you have to do is tick the box beside the answer that best describes why you did not wish to be interviewed, and then send the slip back to us in the pre-paid envelope provided. Your answer will be anonymous.

Thank you very much for your help,

Deborah Ghate
Researcher

---CUT HERE---

Please tick the box next to the main reason or reasons why you did not wish to be interviewed:

You were too busy to spare the time ☐

Personal reasons to do with the subject of the survey ☐

You were worried about confidentiality ☐

You did not understand the reason for the survey ☐

Some other reason **(PLEASE SAY WHAT)** ☐ _____

Please indicate **sex:** Male ☐ Female ☐

age: 18-25 ☐ 26-35 ☐ 36-45 ☐ 46-55 ☐ 56 or over ☐

Phase Four – 48 fully structured interviews

Pre-pilot 4

Phase four involved seven interviewers in a larger scale pre-pilot which was intended as a 'dress-rehearsal' for a true pilot, such as would be carried out before a national survey went into the field. The same areas were used as for pre-pilot 3 with the addition of Newcastle-upon-Tyne. All information gained from the previous phases was combined to produce a fully structured questionnaire, which was used with a pre-selected random sample of addresses in the seven areas. In an effort to minimise deadwood addresses, in the interests of efficiency a PAF sample was simulated by selecting addresses (but not named respondents) from the electoral register, and again, once contact had been made at the address the interviewer selected a potential respondent in the household at random. 48 interviews were achieved.

Callbacks

Once the pre-pilot was finished, a small number of second interviews were carried out by the research team. The purpose of these interviews was to investigate in more detail respondents' perceptions of the survey and the process of being interviewed, as well as to explore issues such as quality and accuracy of recall. Respondents were selected to reflect the mixed nature of the pre-pilot sample in terms of gender, age and childhood sexual history. In total five depth interviews of this type were carried out, varying in length from one to two hours.

Phase Four

Aims:

- to investigate response using chosen method of sampling and chosen approach
- to finalise fully structured questionnaire design
- to investigate in more detail respondents' perceptions of the survey and the process of being interviewed, and to explore issues such as quality and accuracy of recall

Carried out:

- pre-pilot 4 – random (PAF) sample (simulated); 48 fully structured interviews
- depth follow-up interviews with sub-sample of respondents in pre-pilot 4, selected to reflect the mixed nature of the sample in terms of gender, age and childhood sexual history; 5 interviews

Documents used in pre-pilot 4:

- Letter of introduction
- Address Record Form and selection sheet (as pre-pilot 3)
- Comment slip supplied with pre-paid envelope (as pre-pilots 1–3)
- Lists of local counselling and support services (as pre-pilots 1–3)
- Letter sent to respondents selected for follow-up interview

DEPARTMENT OF HEALTH

October 1992

35 NORTHAMPTON SQUARE
LONDON EC1V 0AX
TELEPHONE 071-250 1866

LEARNING ABOUT SEX:
CHILDREN'S EARLY KNOWLEDGE AND EXPERIENCES
A national survey commissioned by the Department of Health, 1992

We would greatly appreciate your help with this survey, which is being carried out by Social and Community Planning Research, an independent research institute, on behalf of the Department of Health.

What is the survey about?

The survey is about adults' memories of their own childhood. It looks at childhood, growing up, and what today's adults learned about sexual development and and sex when they were children. The survey is not about children today; it is being carried out among adults in order to look at changes over time, and to get adults' views about their own childhood experiences.

Why study this subject?

There is little reliable research on this subject for Britain as a whole, yet information of this kind is vital for planning services in areas such as: health and development, sex education, and personal safety for children who may be at risk of unwanted sexual experiences. At present, most of the available research is from other countries, and information from Britain is urgently needed in order to plan future services properly.

How did your address come up?

To carry out a scientific study of this kind, we need to select people entirely at random. If this is not done, there is a risk that the results will be biased. Your address was chosen at random from the electoral register for your area. At your address, the interviewer needs to select one adult in your household to be interviewed, and again, this is done at random. It is very important that as many people as possible who are selected agree to take part- if too many people refuse, the results will not be reliable. It does not matter if there are parts of your childhood which you cannot remember well, we would still like to be able to include you in the research.

Will my answers be kept confidential?

Yes. We take confidentiality very seriously. No information given to the interviewer will be passed on by the research team in such a way as to identify you personally. Your name and address are not put on the questionnaire- we use numbers to protect your anonymity. You will not have to answer any questions you do not wish to.

If you would like further information about the study, you can contact the researchers, Liz Spencer, Deborah Ghate or Bob Erens at SCPR on 071-250 1866.

Yours sincerely,

Liz Spencer   Deborah Ghate   Bob Erens   Wendy Rose
SCPR   SCPR   SCPR   Department of Health

35 NORTHAMPTON SQUARE
LONDON EC1V 0AX
TELEPHONE 071-250 1866
FAX 071-250 1524
E-mail (Janet) : scpr @ uk.ac.city

October 29th 1992

Learning About Sex:
Children's early knowledge and experience

A national survey commissioned by the Department of Health, 1992

Dear

Thank you very much for your kind help with this survey. Your contribution to the research was extremely valuable, and we are pleased to be able to tell you that the survey was very successful, with the majority of people who were contacted agreeing to take part.

As a research team, our work on this study has not yet finished, however. An important part of the process of the survey is for us to look at how well questionnaire actually worked - for example, were the questions clear? Could people remember details about their childhood accurately? How did it feel to be interviewed about a sensitive subject like this? Answers to these questions are vital for us to have, so that we can plan the next stage of the survey, when many more people will be interviewed. To get these answers, we would like to talk to a small cross-section of people a second time.

At the end of the interview, you told the interviewer that you would be willing to talk to us again as part of our research, and I hope you won't mind me writing to ask for your help again with this important stage of the survey.

We would like to come and talk to you again, not to ask the same questions as before, but to help us get a picture of what it felt like to be interviewed. The interview would be carried out by Liz Spencer or Deborah Ghate, from the research team, and there would be a small payment of £12.00 to thank you for your time. We expect that the interview will take about an hour, although it will vary depending on the individual. Once again, the interview will be very informal and everything you say will be treated in the strictest confidence.

Liz Spencer or Deborah Ghate will telephone you in the next few days, and will be pleased to answer any queries you may have about this part of the research. We do hope you will feel able to help us once again.

Yours sincerely

Deborah Ghate
Researcher

Director Roger Jowell, **Deputy Director** Colin Airey.
Department Heads Stephen Elder (Data Processing), Jane Ritchie (Qualitative Research), Marian Stringer (Fieldwork), Roger Thomas (Methods).
Research Directors Lindsay Brook, Pam Campanelli, Paddy Costigan, Gillian Courtenay, Bob Erens, Julia Field, Helen Finch, Jon Hales,
Peter Lynn, Patricia Prescott-Clarke, Patten Smith, Andrew Thomas.
Director of Development Barry Hedges.
Registered as a Charity No. 258538

Response: detailed outcomes

Detailed outcomes can only be listed for pre–pilots 3 and 4, where random sampling methods were used. Table 2 shows the detailed outcomes.

Table 2. **Detailed outcomes pre-pilots 3 and 4**

Pre-pilot 3
Approach (a): 'A survey of childhood and children's knowledge and understanding of sex'
Approach (b): 'A survey of public attitudes to child sexual abuse'
Pre-pilot 4: 'Learning about sex: a survey of children's early knowledge and experiences'

	Pre-pilot 3		Pre-pilot 4
	Approach (a)	Approach (b)	
Issued	112	26	127
Ineligible*	31	4	21
Temporarily unavailable during f/w period	4	5	6
Deadwood	7	2	15
Non-contacts	18	5	17
Refusals	23	1	20
Productive interviews	29	9	48

*Households were classified as ineligible if:
1) they contained no-one aged between 18 and 60 years old, or
2) they contained no-one brought up in the UK (defined as resident by age 4).

Table 3 shows the response rates achieved in pre–pilots 3 and 4. Only the rates for approach (a) are shown, as the sample issued for approach (b) was very small. Because of the short fieldwork periods allowed for the two final

Table 3 **Outcome in pre-pilots 3 and 4: summary data**

	Pre-pilot 3*	Pre-pilot 4
Issued	113	175
Out of scope		
(Ineligibles, unavailable during fieldwork period**, non-contacts, deadwood, unused)	61	107
In scope:	52	68
Refusals	23 (44%)	20 (29%)
Productive interviews	29 (56%)	48 (71%)

* Approach (a) only
**Because of the very short fieldwork period, respondents who were temporarily unavailable for interview during this time were included in the out of scope category. There remains, of course, the possibility that with longer fieldwork periods and continuing unavailability, some of these people would have been recoded to the in scope/refusal category.

pre-pilots, and thus the very limited time available to interviewers in which to make contact at an address, we have calculated response as a proportion of addresses known to be "in scope"; that is, where contact was made and the interviewer was able to establish that there was at least one person resident in the household of eligible age or childhood country of residence. The calculation of response in a full-scale survey would, of course, normally include non-contacts with other unproductive outcomes such as refusals; the proportion of non-contacts, would, however, be expected to be kept to a minimum, as interviewers would be instructed to keep calling at an address throughout the specified period of fieldwork (usually three to four weeks, depending on assignment sizes), in order to achieve contact.

Questionnaire: overview

The design and structure of the questionnaire are discussed in some detail in the main body of this report. Four different versions of the questionnaire were prepared, ranging from a semi-structured to a fully-structured version. A modular design was developed, in which different combinations of modules were phased in and out over the course of the four pre-pilots.

Figure 2 shows the modules included in the questionnaires. Those marked with an asterisk were core modules, used in every version of the questionnaire. The combinations of modules used in each pre-pilot are shown in Table 4.

Figure 2 **the questionnaire**

Establishing context

*Module 1   **Current background/demographic details**

*Module 2   **Childhood circumstances**
                        (household composition, parents' occupation/social class, family
                        finances etc.)

*Module 3   **Childhood family relationships**
                        (parents' relationship, respondent's relationships with key family
                        members)

Module 4   **Other childhood relationships and friendships**

Asking about early sexual knowledge and experience

*Module 5   **First understanding and knowledge of growing up, sexual
                        development and sex**
                        (early impressions of sex and extent of knowledge about sexual
                        matters, attitudes within the home to sexual matters, level/content of
                        formal sex education)

*Module 6   **Childhood sexual experiences**
Separate   (circumstances and content of sexual experiences before 16,
incident form   respondent's perceptions of quality of experience at time and
                        subsequently, whether told anyone else)

*Module 7   **Attempts and narrow escapes before 16**
                        (unsuccessful/uncompleted attempts by others at sexual contact with
                        respondent)

Collecting information about effects and outcomes

*Module 8   **Effects of sexual experiences before 16**
                        (immediate and long term sequelae of early sexual experiences)

Module 9   **Adult sexual experiences**
Self-completion   (sexual contacts since 16, number/gender of partners, whether any
                        coercive experiences, whether any sexual contact with minors)

Module 10   **Life events history**
Self-completion   (checklist of life events before and after 16)

Module 11   **Adult physical and mental health**
                        (physical and mental health problems or disabilities, psychiatric
                        morbidity, contact with therapeutic/counselling services)

Feedback

*Module 12   **Experiences of taking part in the interview**
                        Feelings about taking part in the study, reactions to questions, ease of
                        recall, level of comfort with interviewer, general comments)

Asking about attitudes to child sexual abuse

Module 13   **Attitudes to and awareness of child sexual abuse**
Pre-pilot 3b only   (awareness and understanding of child sexual abuse, estimation of
                        prevalence, attitudes to perpetration.)

---

* denotes core module

Interview Length

The average length of interviews varied across the four pre-pilots depending on the combination of modules included and are given in Table 4 below:

Table 4 **Interview length by pre-pilot**

	Pre-pilot 1 modules 1–8, 12	**Pre-pilot 2** modules 1–9, 11, 12	**Pre-pilot 3(a)** modules 1–8, 10–12	**Pre-pilot 3(b)** modules 1, 6–8, 12, 13	**Pre-pilot 4** modules 1–3, 5–8, 12
Average interview length (minutes)	69	79	65	34	47